TREASURES

IN MY

SPIRITUAL

HOPE CHEST

GOLDEN NUGGETS OF TRUTH

Volume 2

Marjorie Strebe

All Scripture quotations are taken from the Holy Bible, King James Version, Cambridge, 1769.

Published by:
Marjorie Strebe
Trenton, OH 45067

Interior Design by Marjorie Strebe
Treasures in My Spiritual Hope Chest, Volume 2 / Marjorie Strebe
Library of Congress Control Number: 2024917531
ISBN: 979-8-9902136-0-9
Printed in the United States of America

Philippians 2:5

Let this mind be in you, which was also in Christ Jesus.

It's Captivating!

As I reviewed this latest devotional book by Marj, the depth of her insight made it difficult for me to put down.

It is very difficult to use as a daily devotion because it captivates your interest and makes you want to keep reading ahead. I found that it challenged my curiosity to explore the myriad of thoughts that were generated by each segment she shared.

It's like a Thanksgiving dinner that you can't stop eating. This is a book you need in your arsenal of spiritual growth material.

Steve Wilson, Pastor/Author

A Beautiful Journey with God

Treasures in My Spiritual Hope Chest is a delightful devotion full of important information for those of us who want to enjoy sweet fellowship with the Lord in the morning.

Marjorie Strebe takes readers on a beautiful journey with God and His words.

Jacques Alexis, Evangelist
Rawling School of Theology
M.Div. Liberty Theological Seminary
Member of Hilltop Baptist Church, Fairfield, OH

Reaching Upward

Drawing Closer

Marjorie Strebe

Sharing Nuggets of Scriptural Truth

God's Word is an incredible source of information – things that God wants us to know.

It's the greatest Book of history ever written. It explains…

- Where we came from
- How sin entered the world and the result
- The world-wide flood
- The reason there are so many different languages
- God's provision for our salvation

It's a Book of prophecy. It warns about future events...

- The rapture
- The seven-year tribulation period
- The judgment
- The lake of fire
- The millennial reign

It's a Book of instruction. It gives us wise counsel on...

- How to escape hell
- How to please God
- How to live in a way that helps us to stay healthy and happy

It's God's autobiography. It covers...

- God's different names
- God's innumerable attributes
- God's ways
- God's commandments and expectations for mankind

These encouraging words are designed to give you a nugget of truth that will assist your spiritual growth when you apply God's Word to your life. Begin each devotional with prayer, asking for God to guide you throughout this book.

TABLE OF CONTENTS

A Note from the Author

For several years, I discipled a good friend in the things of the Lord. Although she'd been saved for more than twenty years, and she had sat under the teaching of God's word the entire time, she had allowed her spiritual growth to be delayed by circumstances. As a result, she was still young in the Lord. So she always asked the same kinds of questions as baby Christians.

One day she said to me, "You are such a good teacher."

I replied, "A good teacher starts out as a good student."

At that time, I'd been saved and learning how to walk with the Lord for 40 years. When I was still a babe in Christ, I developed an incredible hunger for God. I earnestly sought His will for my life. I listened in church and attempted to apply what I learned to my life. I went from constantly talking to myself to constantly talking to God. He's taught me so much.

But as I reflect on my spiritual infancy, I see how God protected me from false doctrine and guided me into the Truth of His Word. I realize that my early obedience was crucial to my spiritual growth – learning to be faithful to *all* church services (not just Sunday morning), getting baptized, learning to tithe, reading my Bible consistently, memorizing Scripture, going out on visitation, etc.

God was as active in my spiritual growth as I was. And I know there were times when my own stubbornness or rebellion stifled my spiritual development, but I learned of God before I taught another. I was a student before I became a teacher.

A pastor once told me that it was *my responsibility* to disciple the lady I'd led to the Lord – a lady who was perfectly content to remain a spiritual babe. You can't be a teacher when you have no student, and she had no desire to learn and grow. I couldn't even get her to attend church because she feared she'd miss a phone call from her husband, who was on the road with my husband.

For a few years, I worked as an educational assistant at the local school district, and sometimes I worked with children who were severely mentally handicapped – 10 and 11 year old students who were still learning the days of the week and their personal information.

That is not the norm. Most children that age are learning to write essays, spell difficult words, multiply double digits, and have been introduced to algebra. But most of *God's* children seem to have learning disabilities?

A Note from the Author

They haven't learned to read their Bibles, attend Sunday school, pray, or memorize Scripture. They have no desire to obey in the little things, and they don't understand why God doesn't guide them.

If you've been saved for 10...20...30 years, and you are still a baby Christian, know that your obedience is crucial to your spiritual growth.

If you can't obey God in the little things, such as faithful church attendance, don't expect Him to help you in the big things. If *you're* not willing to be actively involved in your spiritual growth, don't expect God to do it. But you'll find that the more you do to draw close to God, obey His Word, and grow in grace, the more He'll do to guide you through the process.

But the spiritual growth aspect of your salvation *begins with you.*

This book is not designed to replace your daily Bible reading, but to supplement it.

Faith

Whatsoever is Not of Faith is Sin

"And he that doubteth is damned if he eat, because he eateth not of faith: for whatsoever is not of faith is sin."

Romans 14:23

Our faith pleases God.

- To believe that God honors His Word...
- To trust Him no matter what happens...
- To have confidence in His love toward us...
- To know that He cannot lie or make a mistake...
- To trust in Jesus without ever seeing him...

How can we not trust One who is so trustworthy?

But to not believe in God...

To not trust in Jesus...

To doubt the Creator ... is to live in perpetual sin.

Jesus is the Creator of all things – visible and invisible (John 1:3).

We frequently place our trust in a fallible person or a man-made product. How much more trustworthy is God Almighty, the infallible One?

Hebrews 11:6 says, **"But without faith it is impossible to please him: for he that cometh to God must believe that he is, and that he is a rewarder of them that diligently seek him."**

In Romans 14:14 Paul says, **"I know, and am persuaded by the Lord Jesus, that there is nothing unclean of itself: but to him that esteemeth any thing to be unclean, to him it is unclean."**

If you think that something is wrong, then it's a sin for you to partake in it. **"For whatsoever is not of faith is sin,"** regardless of what it is.

As a believer, is it wrong or sinful to watch television, go to the movies, or listen to secular music? If you truly think an activity is wrong for you, you're in sin if you partake in any way. That's what it means that **"whatsoever is not of faith is sin."**

But according to the holy Scriptures, we have liberty in Christ.

Galatians 5:13 says, **"For, brethren, ye have been called unto liberty; only use not liberty for an occasion to the flesh..."**

Liberty gives us freedom. But it doesn't give us freedom to feed our lusts and yield to the flesh. There's nothing wrong with enjoying a television program, but if you're spending hours in front of the TV or you're watching programs that glorify sinful choices, you are using your liberty **"for an occasion to the flesh."**

"And he that doubteth is damned if he eat, because he eateth not of faith: for whatsoever is not of faith is sin." Romans 14:23

Faith Comes by Hearing the Word of God

"So then faith cometh by hearing, and hearing by the word of God."

Romans 10:17

God made it easy for you to begin developing a faith that would please Him. You start with His Word. How do you develop faith? By hearing the Word of God. Not just by reading silently, but by hearing God's Word as it is being read.

Isaiah 55:11 says, **"So shall my word be that goeth forth out of my mouth: it shall not return unto me void, but it shall accomplish that which I please, and it shall prosper in the thing whereto I sent it."**

God has a purpose for every word from His Word. And one of those purposes is to develop and strengthen our faith.

That's why Romans 10:17 says, **"So then faith cometh by hearing, and hearing by the word of God."**

Your faith is a crucial part of your Christian walk and growth.

Ephesians 6:16 says, **"Above all, taking the shield of faith, wherewith ye shall be able to quench all the fiery darts of the wicked."**

You're to take the shield of faith and by it, you will extinguish the fiery darts of Satan.

I Thessalonians 5:8 says, **"But let us, who are of the day, be sober, putting on the breastplate of faith and love; and for an helmet, the hope of salvation."**

You're to put on the breastplate of faith and love. It doesn't protect you accidentally. You have to make a conscious decision to shield yourself with both faith and love.

Romans 5:1 says, **"Therefore being justified by faith, we have peace with God through our Lord Jesus Christ."**

You are declared righteous in the sight of God by your faith.

That's why Hebrews 10:38 says, **"Now the just shall live by faith: but if any man draw back, my soul shall have no pleasure in him."**

For these reasons, faith is essential. And although the first step is easy – hearing the Word of God – developing strong faith requires exercising that faith, which is similar to building muscles. Even the strongest body builder started out by learning to hold up his head.

I Timothy 6:12 says, **"Fight the good fight of faith..."**

Developing faith is a fight.

Keeping your faith is a fight.

Everything in the world wants to tear it down.

You must be in God's Word to keep your faith firm and strong.

- In Sunday school
- In preaching services
- In Bible studies
- In personal study and devotions

"So then faith cometh by hearing, and hearing by the word of God."

Faith Overcomes the World

"For whatsoever is born of God overcometh the world: and this is the victory that overcometh the world, even our faith."

I John 5:4

To overcome means "to defeat in competition or conflict; conquer." As children of God, we have the power to conquer the world, and that power comes through our faith. To "overcome the world" means to make good and right decisions that go against the sinful influences that pervade society.

In John 15:19, Jesus said, **"If ye were of the world, the world would love his own: but because ye are not of the world, but I have chosen you out of the world, therefore the world hateth you."**

The world is *not* your friend.

I John 2:15-16 says, **"Love not the world, neither the things that are in the world. If any man love the world, the love of the Father is not in him. For all that is in the world, the lust of the flesh, and the lust of the eyes, and the pride of life, is not of the Father, but is of the world."**

These are the worldly influences that you have the power to overcome through your faith in Christ.

Your faith is only as reliable as the object in which it's placed. In other words, if you place your faith in a person, whether that person is your spouse, your best friend, your boss, or even yourself, your faith will eventually fail because the object of your faith is flawed. Even with the best of intentions, a person is subject to error.

Notice that the verse doesn't say, "whosoever is born of God" but it says, **"whatsoever is born of God."** The whatsoever is your faith. That's why the verse concludes with **"and this is the victory that overcometh the world, even our faith."**

In order to defeat worldly influences in your life, you must place your faith in Christ Jesus, the Savior of the world, and Him alone. Everything else will fail you. You will fail yourself.

- God never makes mistakes.
- God's motives are always pure.
- God's judgments are always just.
- God's decisions are always right.
- God always does what's best for us.

You can safely put your faith in God. He will never fail you, and your faith in Him will help you to conquer the worldly influences in your life.

Forgiveness

Why Forgive

> *"Forbearing one another, and forgiving one another, if any man have a quarrel against any: even as Christ forgave you, so also do ye."*
>
> Colossians 3:13

Why should I forgive after what he did to me?

I don't care if she apologized. She doesn't deserve my forgiveness.

At one time or another, we've all heard someone voice these sentiments, or maybe we've even said them to someone else.

The question is, "Does anyone deserve forgiveness?"

No! Not your spouse or your sibling or your best friend or your neighbor or your brother-in-law or your child ... or YOU! So, then, if no one deserves forgiveness, why should anyone forgive anyone?

Forgiveness begins with God.

Psalm 86:5 says, **"For thou, Lord, art good, and ready to forgive; and plenteous in mercy unto all them that call upon thee."**

I John 1:9 says, **"If we confess our sins, he is faithful and just to forgive us our sins, and to cleanse us from all unrighteousness."**

All sin is an offense against God! Without God's mercy and forgiveness, we stand no chance of getting into Heaven.

In referring to Jesus' death on the cross, Ephesians 1:7 says, **"In whom we have redemption through his blood, the forgiveness of sins, according to the riches of his grace."**

God's grace is a gift. It means that He gives us something that we haven't earned and do not deserve, such as His mercy and forgiveness.

So, then, what gives us the right to withhold our forgiveness from others?

"I forgave him, and he did it again!"

Is there anyone who can go one day without sinning against God? I think not. And if you think you can, then that thought just caused you to sin because of pride.

Do you give thanks for everything on any given day? No one does. We all take certain things for granted. That's a sin, one that we commit every single day. So if God forgives us over and over again for the same things, shouldn't we do the same for others? How do you think God feels when He forgives us, but we won't forgive another? I'll tell you how He feels.

Matthew 6:14-15 says, **"For if ye forgive men their trespasses, your heavenly Father will also forgive you: But if ye forgive not men their trespasses, neither will your Father forgive your trespasses."**

Matthew 18:21-22 says, **"Then came Peter to him, and said, Lord, how oft shall my brother sin against me, and I forgive him? till seven times? Jesus saith unto him, I say not unto thee, Until seven times: but, Until seventy times seven."**

That's a BIG number. Did Jesus intend for us to keep a record so we'd know when to stop forgiving?

In Matthew 18:23-35, Jesus tells the story of a man who refused to forgive a small debt from a fellow servant after his master had already forgiven him of a huge debt.

His master was furious and **"delivered him to the tormentors, till he should pay all that was due unto him."**

Then Jesus said, **"So likewise shall my heavenly Father do also unto you, if ye from your hearts forgive not every one his brother their trespasses."**

This passage clarifies verse 22 because only a few verses later, Jesus tells us to forgive everyone who sins against us. He didn't intend for us to keep a record. He intended for us to forgive others the way God forgives us.

As you can see, God takes forgiveness very seriously.

The Importance of Forgiveness

"And when ye stand praying, forgive, if ye have ought against any: that your Father also which is in heaven may forgive you your trespasses.

But if ye do not forgive, neither will your Father which is in heaven forgive your trespasses."

Mark 11:25-26

Exodus 34:6-7 says, **"And the LORD... proclaimed, The LORD, The LORD God, merciful and gracious, longsuffering, and abundant in goodness and truth, Keeping mercy for thousands, forgiving iniquity and transgression and sin..."**

God is merciful, gracious, and patient. Because of these characteristics, He is always ready to forgive.

Psalm 86:5 says, **"For thou, Lord, art good, and ready to forgive; and plenteous in mercy unto all them that call upon thee."**

So when we come before Him in prayer, we are calling upon Him. And God is listening to our prayers, ready to forgive us if we simply confess our sins and turn from them.

I John 1:9 says, **"If we confess our sins, he is faithful and just to forgive us our sins, and to cleanse us from all unrighteousness."**

That is the God we serve – kind, loving, merciful, full of goodness and truth, and ready to forgive.

If we harbor anger and bitterness in our lives, then we are maintaining a spirit of unforgiveness, and unforgiveness is a sin. How, then, can we expect God to forgive us of our sins when we choose to hold onto an unforgiving spirit?

Proverbs 28:13 says, **"He that covereth his sins shall not prosper: but whoso confesseth and forsaketh them shall have mercy."**

To receive the mercy of God, we must confess and forsake our sins. *All our sins.* That includes the sin of unforgiveness.

And Psalm 66:18 says, **"If I regard iniquity in my heart, the Lord will not hear me."**

That's why Mark 11:26 says, **"But if ye do not forgive, neither will your Father which is in heaven forgive your trespasses."**

There is no forgiveness aside of confession, and if you harbor unconfessed sins, you're choosing not to confess it or forsake it. Therefore, God doesn't hear your prayer, so how can He forgive you when

He doesn't hear a confession or see any form of repentance?

Psalm 32:5 says, **"I acknowledged my sin unto thee, and mine iniquity have I not hid. I said, I will confess my transgressions unto the LORD; and thou forgavest the iniquity of my sin."**

We Forgive for Christ's Sake

> *"And be ye kind one to another, tenderhearted, forgiving one another, even as God for Christ's sake hath forgiven you."*
>
> Ephesians 4:32

God loves you tremendously, and because He loves you, He sent His Son to pay the penalty for your sin.

I John 4:14 says, **"...the Father sent the Son to be the Saviour of the world."**

Since Jesus paid the price for sin, you are forgiven. And God expects you to forgive others **"...even as God for Christ's sake hath forgiven you."**

I John 4:7 says, **"Beloved, let us love one another: for love is of God; and every one that loveth is born of God, and knoweth God."**

When we love others as God loves us, we're tenderhearted and show them kindness, which helps us to forgive as we ought to. And that pleases God.

In Ezekiel 36:26, God says to Israel, **"A new heart also will I give you, and a new spirit will I put within you: and I will take away the stony heart out of your flesh, and I will give you an heart of flesh."**

When you were born again, you became a new creature in Christ.

II Corinthians 5:17 says, **"Therefore if any man be in Christ, he is a new creature: old things are passed away; behold, all things are become new."**

At the moment of salvation, God gives you a new heart and a new spirit. But it's up to you what you do with them. Do you fill your heart and mind with the things of God or do you hang onto your old ways and habits?

But even though you are now a new creature in Christ, the old flesh is still with you. That's why Ephesians 4:22-23 tells us to put off the corrupt and deceitful behavior of the old man, and allow your mind to be renewed. Then you can forgive someone else as Christ forgave you by putting "**on the new man, which after God is created in righteousness and true holiness."** (Ephesians 4:24)

"For we are his workmanship, created in Christ Jesus unto good works, which God hath before ordained that we should walk in them." (Ephesians 2:10)

Let's honor our Heavenly Father by displaying the kind of forgiveness that would glorify Him. After all, he forgave us for Christ's sake. We should also forgive others for Christ's sake.

No Stone Throwing

"Forbearing one another, and forgiving one another, if any man have a quarrel against any: even as Christ forgave you, so also do ye."

Colossians 3:13

We serve a gracious and forgiving God. Who can claim to deserve God's mercy and forgiveness? No one.

Psalm 103:10 says, **"He hath not dealt with us after our sins; nor rewarded us according to our iniquities."**

Our sins have separated us from a holy and righteous God.

"But your iniquities have separated between you and your God, and your sins have hid his face from you, that he will not hear." Isaiah 59:2

God doesn't offer His forgiveness to us because we deserve it but because He's merciful and kind, and He loves us more than we can ever comprehend.

In John 8, a crowd of people brought before Jesus a woman taken in adultery. According to the law, she deserved stoning. Yet, Jesus said to them in verse seven, **"...He that is without sin among you, let him first cast a stone at her."** Then verse 9 says,

Forgiveness

"And they which heard it, being convicted by their own conscience, went out one by one, beginning at the eldest, even unto the last…"

We all sin. We all make mistakes. We all fail. Aren't we glad that God is merciful and forgives us?

When you fail to forgive someone, you actually stand in judgment of that person.

Yet, Matthew 7:1 clearly states, **"Judge not, that ye be not judged."**

And the only one who can stand in judgment of another is one who never sins. That disqualifies the entire human race.

But what about courtroom judges? They judge according to the laws of the land. And to be a judge, you cannot have a criminal background. So someone who breaks the laws of the land can never sit in judgment of another person in a court of law. Therefore, the principle is no different.

Jesus is our ultimate Judge. One day, all believers will stand before Him at *The Judgment Seat of Christ,* and we'll all give an account of our works – what we've done for Christ. (Matthew 25:34-40; Hebrews 6:10; II Corinthians. 5:10)

And the lost will answer to God at *The Great White Throne Judgment,* and they'll all give an account for *their* works – for what they've done for Christ. (Matthew 25:41-46; Revelation 20:11-13)

Remember our verse? **"Forbearing one another, and forgiving one another, if any man have a quarrel against any: even as Christ forgave you, so also do ye."**

God expects us as believers to patiently bear with one another, and if anyone wrongs us, we're to forgive them just like Christ has forgiven us.

Dare we do any different than Christ? If we choose not to forgive, then we elect to stand in judgment of the other person. And judgment belongs to God.

That's why Jesus said, **"...He that is without sin among you, let him first cast a stone at her."**

None of us are so righteous that we can throw stones. So if you are harboring unforgiveness in your heart toward anyone, know for certain that you are disobeying God's Word and your disobedience dishonors the Lord, especially after He's forgiven you of so much.

We're Ambassadors for Christ

"If we confess our sins, he is faithful and just to forgive us our sins, and to cleanse us from all unrighteousness."

I John 1:9

God is gracious and merciful. That's why He forgives over and over again.

In Exodus 34:6-7, God proclaims **"...The LORD, The LORD God, merciful and gracious, longsuffering, and abundant in goodness and truth, Keeping mercy for thousands, forgiving iniquity and transgression and sin..."**

God is so good that He bestows upon you the forgiveness that you don't deserve. However, there is something you must do in order to receive that forgiveness.

You must confess your sins.

That means you admit to God that you sinned. And when you confess to God, he not only forgives you of the sin that you confessed, but He cleanses you from *all* unrighteousness – that includes the sins you may have forgotten about or the sins that you didn't realize were sins.

Then Psalm 103:12 says, **"As far as the east is from the west, so far hath he removed our transgressions from us."**

Hence, you now stand righteous in the sight of God.

People are not as forgiving as God. And often times, we hold onto a grudge because we don't feel that the person who offended us deserves our forgiveness. That may be true. They may deserve your forgiveness no more than you deserve God's forgiveness. But God forgives you anyway. So why does God forgive His children when they often refuse to forgive each other?

My sin offends a holy and righteous God. But God is loving, kind, and gracious; and He cares about me. So if I recognize that I've sinned against Him, and I confess my sin, He promptly forgives me and cleanses me from all unrighteousness. God always does what's best for me; restoring my fellowship with Him and helping me to grow spiritually.

But when someone else's sin offends me, is it still all about me?

How I feel. How I look. How badly I hurt.

Those who refuse to forgive are angry, bitter, resentful, and self-centered. Is that how God wants us to behave?

I Peter 1:15-16 says,**"But as he which hath called you is holy, so be ye holy in all manner of conversation; Because it is written, Be ye holy; for I am holy."**

If a holy God can forgive all those who sin against Him, and we are commanded to be holy in **"all manner of conversation,"** meaning that God expects us to maintain godly behavior and a holy lifestyle, then we have a responsibility to show mercy and forgiveness to others like our Savior displays toward us.

II Corinthians 5:20 says, **"Now then we are ambassadors for Christ…"**

As believers, we represent Christ in all we do. Let us, therefore, exemplify the mercy of God in our lives.

"And be ye kind one to another, tenderhearted, forgiving one another, even as God for Christ's sake hath forgiven you." (Ephesians 4:32)

Peace

Loving God's Law Brings Peace

"Great peace have they which love thy law: and nothing shall offend them."

Psalm 119:165

Peace is available to each and every one of God's precious children. God's peace blesses you with a mental calm that frees you from fear; and a tranquil heart that allows you to rest securely in the assurance of His love and protection.

But Jesus gives us more than peace. He desires that we experience *great* peace.

Philippians 4:7 says, **"And the peace of God, which passeth all understanding, shall keep your hearts and minds through Christ Jesus."**

"Which passeth all understanding" means that it's beyond human comprehension. Only Jesus can understand it. That is *great peace*, and we can only receive it through Christ.

But although God's peace is available to all believers, many of God's people are continually filled with anxiety and turmoil. They don't experience the peace that Jesus promised in John 14:27 when He said ...

"Peace I leave with you, my peace I give unto you: not as the world giveth, give I unto you. Let not your heart be troubled, neither let it be afraid."

Jesus promised to give us His peace and assured us that our hearts need not be troubled or afraid. But that kind of peace comes with a price.

Psalm 119:165 says, **"Great peace have they which love thy law…"**

The price of God's peace is a love for His law. How do we demonstrate that love?

- By taking time to learn and understand His commandments.
- By studying and memorizing His precious Scripture.
- By obeying His Word.

If God's people do those things, they will experience great peace – a peace which is beyond human comprehension, **"…and nothing shall offend them."**

Jesus Gives Us His Peace

"Peace I leave with you, my peace I give unto you: not as the world giveth, give I unto you. Let not your heart be troubled, neither let it be afraid."

John 14:27

There is no greater peace in all the world than the peace that comes from God. Jesus, who is no less than God incarnate, said that He's leaving peace with us. Not just any peace; He's giving us His peace.

The dictionary defines peace as "quiet, tranquility, mental calm."

Jesus gives us a quiet spirit. Psalm 4:8 says, **"I will both lay me down in peace, and sleep: for thou, LORD, only makest me dwell in safety."**
Jesus offers us a tranquil soul. Psalm 46:10 says, **"Be still, and know that I am God: I will be exalted among the heathen, I will be exalted in the earth."**
Jesus provides us with a calm mind. Philippians 4:7 says, **"And the peace of God, which passeth all understanding, shall keep your hearts and minds through Christ Jesus."**

The peace that Jesus provides is calming, assuring, and lasting. It's not like the world's peace

".... not as the world giveth, give I unto you. Let not your heart be troubled, neither let it be afraid." (John 14:27)

What kind of peace does the world have to offer? Money? Friends? Possessions? These things may soothe you for awhile, but the calming effects are short-lived. At its best, the world can only offer you something to dull the pain: drugs, alcohol, or work. And none of these things provides peace. They actually cause tribulation because they are of the world.

In John 16:33, Jesus said, **"These things I have spoken unto you, that in me ye might have peace. In the world ye shall have tribulation: but be of good cheer; I have overcome the world."**

The "peace" of the world only brings trouble and fear. That's why Jesus said, **"Let not your heart be troubled, neither let it be afraid."** (John 14:27)

So, then, how do we live in that peace from day to day when we're constantly surrounded by the things of this world?

Jesus said, **"In the world ye shall have tribulation: but be of good cheer; I have overcome the world."** (John 16:33)

And if Jesus has overcome the world, He makes it possible for us to overcome the world. How?

- By living in the presence of God. **"Thou wilt keep him in perfect peace, whose mind is stayed on thee: because he trusteth in thee."** Isaiah 26:3
- By living in obedience to God. **"Great peace have they which love thy law: and nothing shall offend them."** Psalm 119:165

Peace Only Comes from God

"I will both lay me down in peace, and sleep: for thou, LORD, only makest me dwell in safety."

Psalm 4:8

Your feelings of safety and security come only from God's peace. The peace of God allows you to rest in the assurance of His security, whether you are at work, at play, or preparing to go to bed. And the only place you will find that peace is in the Lord.

Psalm. 29:11 says, **"The LORD will give strength unto his people; the LORD will bless his people with peace."**

Jesus said, **"These things I have spoken unto you, that in me ye might have peace. In the world ye shall have tribulation: but be of good cheer; I have overcome the world."** (John 16:33)

Only the Lord brings peace into our lives. But where does God's peace come from? How do we acquire it?

Through the Holy Spirit of God...

- Romans 14:17 **"For the kingdom of God is not meat and drink; but righteousness, and peace, and joy in the Holy Ghost."**
- Galatians 5:22 **"But the fruit of the Spirit is love, joy, peace..."**

By allowing God to influence our thoughts and actions through His Word...

- Romans 8:6 **"For to be carnally minded is death; but to be spiritually minded is life and peace."**
- Isaiah 54:13 **"And all thy children shall be taught of the LORD; and great shall be the peace of thy children."**

From God Himself...

- I Thessalonians 5:23 **"And the very God of peace sanctify you wholly ..."**
- II Thessalonians 3:16 **"Now the Lord of peace himself give you peace always by all means. The Lord be with you all."**

We serve a God of peace, who desires that His children be filled with His peace, despite a world filled with tribulation and turmoil.

Pride

Stop That Tornado!

> *"These six things doth the LORD hate: yea, seven are an abomination unto him:*
>
> *A proud look, a lying tongue, and hands that shed innocent blood..."*
>
> Proverbs 6:16-17

Hate, abomination: those are strong words, and at the front of God's list of abominations is **"a proud look."** It's even more loathsome to the Lord than murder; for **"hands that shed innocent blood"** is third on the list. Why is that? Why does God place pride on his list as number one – the thing He hates worst of all?

To understand that, you must first catch a glimpse of God's holiness and power. When we see God for who He really is, only then do we begin to recognize our helpless condition.

We can't control the weather or prevent an earthquake.

We can't make our crops grow. We can't live without oxygen or water or heat from the sun, and we have no ability to manufacture these for our survival.

We have no power to heal. Doctors and medicine only help the healing process. God has given the human body an amazing ability to heal itself, to repair broken bones, to fight off infection and certain diseases. Yet He has the power to halt the healing process at any time.

So then, what are we capable of doing without God? Nothing!

Jesus said in John 15:5, **"...without me ye can do nothing."** (By the way, Jesus is God. John 1:1-3)

Due to God's incredible, never-ending love and mercy, He gives you the health, physical strength, and stamina to do whatever you need to do in this life, whether or not you believe in Him and recognize Him as the source.

That's how you go to work each day or take care of your family or enjoy recreational activities or attend school or volunteer. This list is as endless as God's strength and power. So if God is our source of strength and power, what have we to boast about?

When you have pride in yourself without recognizing the ability, health, and strength given you by God, which enables you to accomplish the things that you desire, then you've elevated yourself above your Creator and Lord. By your attitude, you've basically told God that you did it by yourself. You didn't need Him or anything He has to offer.

That's what Lucifer did when he said in Isaiah 14:13 **"... I will exalt my throne above the stars of God ..."**

Lucifer was a created being, but somewhere along the line, he decided that it was now all about him. And just like pride made Satan believe that it was now all about him, human pride deceives us into thinking of ourselves more highly than we ought to.

Romans 12:3 says, **"For I say, through the grace given unto me, to every man that is among you, not to think of himself more highly than he ought to think; but to think soberly, according as God hath dealt to every man the measure of faith."**

We believe our own press, so to speak.

So then, why does God despise pride?

- It causes people to elevate themselves above Him, which means they don't recognize their need for a Savior; hence, they die and go to hell.
- It keeps people in bondage to bitterness and unforgiveness.
- It causes people to lie. (Jesus is the Truth. John 14:6)

- It causes people to live self-centered lives, and others suffer tremendously as a result of the sin spawned from selfish actions: abused and neglected children, bullying, etc.

Due to the selfishness and greed birthed by pride, crime runs rampant, even murder from **"hands that shed innocent blood."**

That's why there's nothing God hates worse than pride! It is the forerunner of every other sin.

Worldly Wisdom is Foolishness to God

> *"Seest thou a man wise in his own conceit? there is more hope of a fool than of him."*
>
> Proverbs 26:12

God has a purpose and a plan for each of His children. But if we are full of conceit and worldly wisdom, we are not vessels that He can use for His honor and glory. because we're too focused on our glory – looking good, reaping the praise of men, flaunting our abilities, etc.

I Corinthians 3:19-20 says, **"For the wisdom of this world is foolishness with God … And again, The Lord knoweth the thoughts of the wise, that they are vain."**

If the wisdom of this world is foolishness and the thoughts of the wise are empty, where's our glory? We have none, so we have nothing to boast about.

Here's what God wants us to do: **"Be of the same mind one toward another. Mind not high things, but condescend to men of low estate. Be not wise in your own conceits."** Romans 12:16

If we humble ourselves before God, His mighty hand will exalt us in His timing. (I Peter 5:6). Then we'll discover that through His power we're able to do great things for Him.

Remember what Jesus said in John 15:5 **"...without me ye can do nothing."**

Wow! God says that there is more hope of a fool than a conceited person. And the Bible tells us what God thinks of fools.

- Fools deny the existence of God.
- Fools are corrupt and commit horrendous sins.

Psalm 53:1 says, **"The fool hath said in his heart, There is no God. Corrupt are they, and have done abominable iniquity: there is none that doeth good."**

Where will this mindset lead them?

- Fools mock sin. (Proverbs 14:9)
- Fools enjoy folly. (Proverbs 15:21)
- Fools disregard the teaching of our Savior.

Matthew 7:26-27 says, **"And every one that heareth these sayings of mine, and doeth them not, shall be likened unto a foolish man, which built his house upon the sand: And the rain descended, and the floods came, and the winds blew, and beat upon that house; and it fell: and great was the fall of it."**

And yet, God says that there is more hope for a fool than for someone full of conceit. Does that tell us how much God abhors the vanity and egotistical attitudes of our pride?

But Proverbs 3:7 gives us some wise instruction. **"Be not wise in thine own eyes: fear the LORD, and depart from evil."**

Before Honor is Humility

"Before destruction the heart of man is haughty, and before honour is humility."

Proverbs 18:12

Everyone likes to be honored; to receive glory, high respect, and recognition for their individual achievements or contribution to a successful project. But the accolades of men quickly dissolve, and your achievements are forgotten by all but a very few.

Yet God declares **"before honour is humility."**

The Easton Bible Dictionary defines humility as "a prominent Christian grace, which is a state of mind well pleasing to God; it preserves the soul in tranquility, and makes us patient under trials."

Is there anything more desirous than peace, which equates to a tranquil heart.

I Timothy 6:6 says, **"But godliness with contentment is great gain."**

To be content is to have peace in your surroundings and circumstances. That comes with a humble heart and spirit. Christ, our Lord and Savior, the God of all creation, was our ultimate example in humility.

In Luke 22:27, Jesus said, **"For whether is greater, he that sitteth at meat, or he that serveth? is not he that sitteth at meat? but I am among you as he that serveth."**

- He washed the feet of His disciples.
- He healed the sick and raised the dead.
- He strengthened the weary.
- He preached the Gospel to the lost.
- He submitted Himself to the Father's will.

Philippians 2:8-10 says, **"And being found in fashion as a man, he humbled himself, and became obedient unto death, even the death of the cross. Wherefore God also hath highly exalted him, and given him a name which is above every name: That at the name of Jesus every knee should bow, of things in heaven, and things in earth, and things under the earth."**

Because He lived a humble and obedient life, salvation was made available to all mankind. His sacrifice should be a continual reminder of our sins. That reminder is humbling, but it is the only way to honor. And God's greatest promises are given to the humble. What an incredible paradox God initiated when He declared that humility is the pathway to glory.

And while humility leads to honor, haughtiness leads to destruction.

Proverbs 18:12 says, **"Before destruction the heart of man is haughty ..."**

Haughty means arrogantly self-admiring and disdainful.

Revelation 3:17 says, **"Because thou sayest, I am rich, and increased with goods, and have need of nothing; and knowest not that thou art wretched, and miserable, and poor, and blind, and naked."**

And yet, that's the attitude and mentality that our society promotes: self esteem, pride. It's all about me and how I view myself. And that philosophy leads to haughtiness.

But Paul says in Romans 12:3, **"For I say, through the grace given unto me, to every man that is among you, not to think of himself more highly than he ought to think; but to think soberly, according as God hath dealt to every man the measure of faith."**

God instructs us to be humble. Jesus was our example, and He expects us to follow it. And for those who do, God blesses them greatly.

- Proverbs 29:23 **"A man's pride shall bring him low: but honour shall uphold the humble in spirit."**
- Matthew 18:4 **"Whosoever therefore shall humble himself as this little child, the same is greatest in the kingdom of heaven."**

- Luke 14:11 **"For whosoever exalteth himself shall be abased; and he that humbleth himself shall be exalted."**
- James 4:6 **"But he giveth more grace. Wherefore he saith, God resisteth the proud, but giveth grace unto the humble."**
- James 4:10 **"Humble yourselves in the sight of the Lord, and he shall lift you up."**

To the believer, humility is far more important than self-esteem. True humility is when we recognize our genuine condition, seeing our wretchedness through the eyes of God.

Without God, we're contemptible and corrupt. God wants us to realize that, and until we do, He can't use us because the opposite of humility is pride.

So if you're not humble, you're proud. And a proud person does things His own way; not God's.

Pride Brings Shame

> *"When pride cometh, then cometh shame: but with the lowly is wisdom."*
>
> Proverbs 11:2

According to the dictionary, "lowly" means humble in feeling, behavior, and status.

Proverbs 16:19 says, **"Better it is to be of an humble spirit with the lowly, than to divide the spoil with the proud."**

God blesses those that humble themselves before Him. He blesses them with wisdom.

Proverbs 15:33 says, **"The fear of the LORD is the instruction of wisdom; and before honour is humility."**

He blesses them with knowledge and understanding.

Proverbs 2:6 says, **"For the LORD giveth wisdom: out of his mouth cometh knowledge and understanding."**

He blesses them with riches, honor, and life.

Proverbs 22:4 says, **"By humility and the fear of the LORD are riches, and honour, and life."**

People don't like to humble themselves before others, especially the Lord, because they consider humility a weakness. If humility is a weakness, then is pride a strength? Not according to God. Mankind may consider pride a strength, but God calls it an abomination. (Proverbs 6:16-17)

Why does God hate pride?

1) It's sin. (Proverbs 21:4)
2) It brings shame. (Proverbs 11:2)
3) It brings a person down. (Proverbs 29:23)
4) It causes contention. (Proverbs 13:10)
5) It brings persecution (Psalm 10:2)
6) It stirs up strife. (Proverbs 28:25)
7) It brings destruction. (Proverbs 16:18)

Pride is an egotistical view of oneself, one's position, or status. Pride causes a person to rely totally on himself – his strength, his power, his ability, his intelligence, his knowledge, and his wisdom. But those things are all a gift from God, which means that in and of ourselves we have nothing to boast of.

Galatians 6:3 says, **"For if a man think himself to be something, when he is nothing, he deceiveth himself."**

When we humble ourselves before God, we recognize that our strength, power, ability, intelligence, knowledge, and wisdom all come from

Him, and we acknowledge that without Christ we could do nothing (John 15:5). So our power is actually in Christ through a humble spirit.

James 4:6 says, **"But he giveth more grace. Wherefore he saith, God resisteth the proud, but giveth grace unto the humble."**

Pride Goes Before Destruction

"Pride goeth before destruction, and an haughty spirit before a fall."

Proverbs 16:18

God honors those who humble themselves before him.

James 4:10 says, **"Humble yourselves in the sight of the Lord, and he shall lift you up."**

When you display humility toward God, you recognize Him for who He really is: the Almighty Creator of the universe. But you also recognize yourself for what you really are: weak and helpless before Almighty God. Therefore, when you humble yourself before God, you allow Him to lift you up, and He can elevate you more effectively than you could yourself.

Proverbs 22:4 says, **"By humility and the fear of the LORD are riches, and honour, and life."**

Most people think that personal pride helps them to succeed in life, but God says that true success comes through humility and the fear of the Lord. So if you humble yourself before the Lord, He will bless you with riches, honor, and life; and He will lift you up.

People cherish their pride. Rich people believe that their pride brought them to this place of prosperity and wealth, while poor people think that's all they have to hold onto. "We may not be wealthy, but at least we have our pride."

Proverbs 29:23 says, **"A man's pride shall bring him low: but honour shall uphold the humble in spirit."**

Whether you are rich or poor (or somewhere in between) pride only brings you down.

What exactly is pride? Pride is elevating yourself above others. A lot of people even exalt themselves above Jesus, our Savior and Creator.

Yet Romans 12:3 says, **"For I say…to every man that is among you, not to think of himself more highly than he ought to think…"**

Why not? What does it hurt to think highly of myself? *That's pride.*

- Pride got Satan kicked out of Heaven. Isaiah 14:12-13 says, **"How art thou fallen from heaven, O Lucifer…For thou hast said in thine heart, I will ascend into heaven, I will exalt my throne above the stars of God…"**

- Pride is sin. Proverbs 21:4 says, **"An high look, and a proud heart, and the plowing of the wicked, is sin."**
- Pride brings shame. Proverbs 11:2 says, **"When pride cometh, then cometh shame: but with the lowly is wisdom."**
- Pride causes contention. Proverbs 13:10 says, **"Only by pride cometh contention: but with the well advised is wisdom."**
- Pride keeps us in a sinful state, preventing mankind from trusting Christ as Savior. Ephesians 2:8-9 says, **"For by grace are ye saved through faith; and that not of yourselves: it is the gift of God: Not of works, lest any man should boast."**
- Pride sends people to hell. Revelation 20:15 says, **"And whosoever was not found written in the book of life was cast into the lake of fire."**
- Pride precedes destruction. Proverbs 16:18 says, **"Pride goeth before destruction, and an haughty spirit before a fall."**

The opposite of pride is humility. Few people today teach on the importance of humility because they have the mistaken idea that humility is synonymous with "doormat," or letting others trample you – emotionally and spiritually. That's the doctrine of the devil, the father of lies.

Look again at the result of pride:

- It is sin.
- It causes contention and shame.
- It brings destruction, thereby keeping people in a sinful state and sending them to hell.
- And its originator got kicked out of Heaven because of it.

Does that sound like a philosophy that will benefit mankind? No! And yet society is sold on the importance of self esteem and personal pride. It's taking our nation straight to hell.

God's word talks about the humble while the devil roams the earth seeking whom he may devour through their pride. And he has lots of volunteers chomping at the bit. God, on the other hand, lifts up the humble.

Jesus said in Matthew 18:4, **"Whosoever therefore shall humble himself as this little child, the same is greatest in the kingdom of heaven."**

Purity

God Expects Us to be Pure

"Beloved, now are we the sons of God, and it doth not yet appear what we shall be: but we know that, when he shall appear, we shall be like him; for we shall see him as he is.

And every man that hath this hope in him purifieth himself, even as he is pure."

I John 3:2-3

Purity means uncorrupted; free from sin.

Christ is pure, and at the moment of the rapture – the instant He appears – we will be like Him. We will be pure and sinless, holy and incorruptible. Yet verse three tells us that everyone who has this hope in himself will purify himself.

Now! In this life!

But why do we need to battle our old sin nature to try and be like Him *now*?

Because God tells us to.

We were made:

To have fellowship with God. God is pure, so our impurities separate us from His fellowship. (Isaiah 59:2)

To commune with God. Because God is pure, He cannot hear us when we maintain impure thoughts and actions. (Psalm 66:18)

To please God. God is pure, so in our naturally sinful state, there is nothing in *our* lives pleasing to Him. (Romans 3:10-18; 8:6-8)

Yet, I John 3:3 instructs us to purify ourselves and I Peter 1:16 tells us to be holy. We can't fellowship with God, commune with God, or in any way please God if we are not pure and holy.

I've heard people say that the reason God wants us to be pure here is to prepare us for Heaven; that if we don't purify ourselves in this life, we won't be comfortable in our Heavenly home.

That makes absolutely no sense. God wants us to purify ourselves here and now because...

- We represent Him, and He is holy
- We bear the name of Christ
- He desires to fellowship with us
- He longs to commune with us
- It pleases Him when we obey

God expects us to be pure.

How to Cleanse Yourself from Sin

> *"Every word of God is pure: he is a shield unto them that put their trust in him.*
>
> *Add thou not unto his words, lest he reprove thee, and thou be found a liar."*
>
> Proverbs 30:5-6

We serve a holy God who is pure in every aspect of His nature. His words flow from His nature. Therefore, God's words are as pure as He.

Psalm 12:6 says, **"The words of the Lord are pure words: as silver tried in a furnace of fire, purified seven times."**

But God's Word isn't only pure. God's Word is also a purifying agent.

Psalm 119:9-11 says, **"Wherewithal shall a young man cleanse his way? by taking heed thereto according to thy word. With my whole heart have I sought thee: O let me not wander from thy commandments. Thy word have I hid in mine heart, that I might not sin against thee."**

Because God's Word is pure, I can cleanse my way by simply obeying it. But if I go a step further –

meditate on God's Word; internalize its message – that will help keep me from sin.

Purified water means that there are no impurities in your drinking water. In other words, there is not the slightest trace of impurities; otherwise, it can't be called "purified" water.

Although God made man in His image, due to Adam's sin, the lost world now battles a sin nature and the saved battles this old flesh. Therefore, mankind is infested with impurities of every kind.

Yet, is our "purified" drinking water purified seven times, as is God's Word? Probably not. Our "purified" water is probably not nearly as pure as we'd like to think. And here we are, full of impurities ourselves, adding and changing God's Holy Word to "clarify" it for easy understanding.

Can God's Holy Word, which He purified seven times, remain pure when it is altered, changed, and reworded by a people, who are, in God's eyes, deceitful and desperately wicked? (Jeremiah 17:9) How can something that is so utterly filthy rub off on something that is spotlessly pure and clean without contaminating it? By our very nature, mankind is impure. If man in any way alters God's words, he has just corrupted the purified Word of God with impurities. How, then, can God's children cling to such corrupted bibles as:

Purity

- The Living Bible – a paraphrase where God's holy words have been changed
- The Amplified Bible – Someone has corrupted the Holy Words of God (which He purified seven times) by adding to it.

Proverbs 30:6 says, **"Add thou not unto his words, lest he reprove thee, and thou be found a liar."**

Revelation 22:18 says, **"For I testify unto every man that heareth the words of the prophecy of this book, If any man shall add unto these things, God shall add unto him the plagues that are written in this book:"**

Is mankind not concerned about the horrendous consequences awaiting the ones who tamper with God's Holy Word?

- NIV – Missing and changed verses. (Compare Acts 8:37 with the KJV)
- ASV – Missing words and changed verses (Compare Romans 8:1 with the KJV)

Compare any other version with the Authorized King James translation of God's Holy Word and you will find missing verses, added words, gross discrepancies in meaning, and horrendous contradictions.

And people flock to these artificial bibles filled with contradictions because the pride of impure people are going to "improve" on the purified Words of God. All they did was contaminate it. No wonder non-Christians say, "The Bible is full of contradictions." And man's revisions are, but God's Holy Word is not.

Revelation 22:19 says, **"And if any man shall take away from the words of the book of this prophecy, God shall take away his part out of the book of life, and out of the holy city, and from the things which are written in this book."**

I've heard people say, "That's just talking about Revelation."

Are you sure? Let's suppose you're right. Have you seen any other version of the Bible that did not also reword the book of Revelation? If you want to purify your heart and life through God's Holy Word, then you must hold fast to the King James Version which has stood the test of time. All other versions are full of impurities and contradictions because mankind has changed God's purified words to "clarify" His meaning, as if they know the mind of God.

The Pure in Heart

"Blessed are the pure in heart: for they shall see God."

Matthew 5:8

What does it mean to be "pure in heart?"

Pure means undefiled and without sin. Jesus is the only person who ever lived that is pure. But Jesus wasn't talking about Himself when He said that the pure in heart shall see God. He was talking about those who put their trust in Him.

Jeremiah 17:9 says, **"The heart is deceitful above all things, and desperately wicked: who can know it"**

That is the heart of the natural man – the lost individual who doesn't know Christ. He only has wickedness in his heart.

Yet, in Luke 6:45, Jesus said, **"A good man out of the good treasure of his heart bringeth forth that which is good; and an evil man out of the evil treasure of his heart bringeth forth that which is evil: for of the abundance of the heart his mouth speaketh."**

But individuals who have placed their faith and trust in Jesus has the Holy Spirit of God dwelling within them, and the Holy Spirit can *only be good.*

So when Jesus says, **"A good man out of the good treasure of his heart bringeth forth that which is good…"** He's referring to that individual who has trusted Him as Savior.

Hebrews 12:14 says, **"Follow peace with all men, and holiness, without which no man shall see the Lord."**

In other words, to be "pure in heart" means to have the Holy Spirit dwelling in your heart so that you are at peace with all men and have the holiness of God dwelling within you. Without that, nobody shall see the Lord.

Christ is pure, so the Christ dwelling within me is pure. Therefore, only those who know Christ as Savior will see God.

Rebellion

Our Ultimate Authority

*"**Foolishness is bound in the heart of a child; but the rod of correction shall drive it far from him.**"*

Proverbs 22:15

The dictionary definition of rebellion is "open resistance to authority," and authority is "the power or right to enforce obedience." There are many today who have that power: our government, law enforcement, most parents, some schools.

There was a day that all parents had that power and the great majority of them gave it to their child's teacher, but the government is working to strip them of all authority by enacting legislation known as "The Rights of the Child."

It sounds good on the surface, but "The Rights of the Child" basically means that the child has the right to decide what's in their best interest, and no one can make them do something they don't want to do, such as attend church or school, do chores around the house, show respect or consideration to others, share, eat their veggies, etc.

But Who is our ultimate Authority? God Almighty. God gives parents the responsibility of bringing up their children in the nurture and admonition of the Lord. (Ephesians 6:4) Admonition means to advise, warn, and rebuke.

Proverbs 22:6 says, **"Train up a child in the way he should go: and when he is old, he will not depart from it."**

Why would God tell parents to train up their children in the way they should go if the children already know what's best for them?

Proverbs 29:15 says, **"The rod and reproof give wisdom: but a child left to himself bringeth his mother to shame."**

A child left to himself brings shame on his mother? Yet, "The Rights of the Child" advocates that we do just that. Too few parents are in favor of neither the rod, nor reproof. They let their children do whatever they choose. In other words, they leave their children to themselves. The result is bullying, school shootings, gang activity, and juvenile crime. These activities are enough to shame any parent. Leaving a child to himself certainly doesn't promote wisdom and honor.

Romans 13:1-2 says, **"Let every soul be subject unto the higher powers. For there is no power but of God: the powers that be are ordained of God. Whosoever therefore resisteth the power, resisteth the ordinance of God..."**

Rebellion

Every person is subject to God's authority, and since all human authority is from God, we're required to obey that, too.

That's why God says in Colossians 3:20, **"Children, obey your parents in all things: for this is well pleasing unto the Lord."**

As far as God's concerned, children have the same responsibilities as the rest of us: to obey those in authority over them.

Let's stand against "The Rights of the Child." It promotes rebellion.

All Rebellion is Against the Lord

> *"For I know thy rebellion, and thy stiff neck: behold, while I am yet alive with you this day, ye have been rebellious against the LORD; and how much more after my death?"*
>
> Deuteronomy 31:27

Romans 5:6-8 says, **"For when we were yet without strength, in due time Christ died for the ungodly. For scarcely for a righteous man will one die: yet peradventure for a good man some would even dare to die. But God commendeth his love toward us, in that, while we were yet sinners, Christ died for us."**

God loved us enough to send His only begotten Son to die for us, even while we were in a continuous state of rebellion against Him. But once we know Christ as Savior, we are to honor God with our worship, praise, and obedience.

Ephesians 5:2 says, **"And walk in love, as Christ also hath loved us, and hath given himself for us an offering and a sacrifice to God for a sweetsmelling savour."**

After all, He spared us from eternal darkness and everlasting torment. That's something to rejoice in.

Psalm 78:7-8 says, **"That they might set their hope in God, and not forget the works of God, but keep his commandments: And might not be as their fathers, a stubborn and rebellious generation; a generation that set not their heart aright, and whose spirit was not stedfast with God."**

It was God's hope that Israel would set their hope in Him and not forget His works, but that they would keep His commandments. Yet time and time again, they rebelled against God.

According to the dictionary, rebellion means open resistance to authority. God is the ultimate authority – not just Israel's authority, but all of creation is to obey Him. The lost don't understand that. They are slaves to sin and simply follow their lusts. Are they living in rebellion? Yes, whether or not they realize it. But God's children are called to higher standards – to a life of holiness and obedience.

Consider how God views rebellion.

I Samuel 15:23 says, **"For rebellion is as the sin of witchcraft, and stubbornness is as iniquity and idolatry…"**

Stubbornness is just as bad as rebellion. God refers to the stubborn as stiff-necked because they refuse to yield to Him.

Proverbs 6:16-19 says, **These six things doth the LORD hate: yea, seven are an abomination unto him:**

- A proud look,
- A lying tongue,
- And hands that shed innocent blood,
- An heart that deviseth wicked imaginations,
- Feet that be swift in running to mischief,
- A false witness that speaketh lies,
- And he that soweth discord among brethren.

Number one on that list is pride, and every sin listed is a form of rebellion that stems from a proud heart.

Before rebellion is pride!

In Isaiah 14:13-14, Satan said in his heart, **"...I will ascend into Heaven, I will exalt my throne above the stars of God: I will sit also upon the mount of the congregation, in the sides of the north: I will ascend above the heights of the clouds; I will be like the most high."**

Is there any doubt in our minds that Satan's pride has led to more evil than anything on this earth?

Rebellion is downright wicked in the eyes of God and all rebellion starts with a proud heart.

"He, that being often reproved hardeneth his neck, shall suddenly be destroyed, and that without remedy." Proverbs 29:1

Rebellion is Comparable to Witchcraft

"For rebellion is as the sin of witchcraft, and stubbornness is as iniquity and idolatry. Because thou hast rejected the word of the LORD, he hath also rejected thee from being king."

I Samuel 15:23

In the eyes of God, rebellion is a horrendous sin, every bit as evil as witchcraft. But through Christ, there is forgiveness.

God's children are not normally involved in witchcraft, but can we rightly claim that we're not rebellious? Rebellion is opposition to authority, and God is our ultimate authority. If we've ever disobeyed God, then we've acted in rebellion. However, we serve a gracious and merciful God.

Micah 7:18 says, **"Who is a God like unto thee, that pardoneth iniquity, and passeth by the transgression of the remnant of his heritage? he retaineth not his anger for ever, because he delighteth in mercy."**

God is forgiving, and he desires to forgive us even when we're rebellious.

Isaiah 55:7 says, **"Let the wicked forsake his way, and the unrighteous man his thoughts: and let him return unto the LORD, and he will have mercy upon him; and to our God, for he will abundantly pardon."**

Even when we've disobeyed and resisted His authority (rebelled against Him), He loves and forgives us. But to receive that forgiveness, we must abandon our evil ways and recommit ourselves to the Lord; to honor and obey Him by our words and deeds. Then, and only then, will He abundantly pardon.

God does not tolerate rebellion, and stubbornness is the main ingredient of a rebellious heart and attitude. Consider what the Bible says...

"For rebellion is as the sin of witchcraft..."

Rebellion means opposition to or defiance of authority. If we defy God's authority by disobeying Him or we simply demonstrate opposition to His Word by our lifestyle, we are living a life of rebellion.

"...and stubbornness is as iniquity and idolatry..."

Stubborn means unreasonably and obstructively determined to persevere or prevail. Are you stubborn? Do you fight God at every turn because you are unreasonably determined to prevail against

Him? You won't. And your stubbornness is equivalent to idol worship.

"Wait a minute, I may be a little stubborn sometimes, but I don't worship idols."

According to God's word, there's no difference between the two.

In Acts 7:51, Stephen said, **"Ye stiffnecked and uncircumcised in heart and ears, ye do always resist the Holy Ghost: as your fathers did, so do ye."**

God's people were stubborn. They resisted the Holy Ghost. That means they rebelled against God, and it all begins with stubbornness. But stubbornness and rebellion are sins like any other. However, God grants forgiveness with repentance,

II Chronicles 30:8 says, **"Now be ye not stiffnecked, as your fathers were, but yield yourselves unto the LORD, and enter into his sanctuary, which he hath sanctified for ever: and serve the LORD your God..."**

Although God was talking to the children of Israel in this verse, the principle applies to us today. He wants His children to serve Him with tender hearts, yielded to His will, guidance, and direction.

Don't be stubborn. Stubbornness leads to rebellion, and God considers rebellion comparable to the sin of witchcraft.

Woe to God's Rebellious Children

"Woe to the rebellious children, saith the LORD, that take counsel, but not of me; and that cover with a covering, but not of my spirit, that they may add sin to sin..."

Isaiah 30:1

In this verse, God is referring to Israel; but it applies just as much to His church today. You see...

- *God loves His children.* I John 3:16 says, **"Hereby perceive we the love of God, because he laid down his life for us: and we ought to lay down our lives for the brethren."**
- *He cares for His children.* I Peter 5:7 says, **"Casting all your care upon him; for he careth for you."**
- *He provides wise counsel to His children.* Psalm 73:24 says, **"Thou shalt guide me with thy counsel, and afterward receive me to glory."**
- *He guides His children with His Holy Spirit.* John 14:16 says, **"And I will pray the Father, and he shall give you another Comforter, that he may abide with you for ever..."**

He does all these things for us. How do we show our appreciation?

Rebellion is a choice that we revel in. How often have we heard someone say, "Rules were made to be broken." If rules were made to be broken, why were they made in the first place? No parent makes rules just for their child to break them. They create rules for the health and well-being of their children and fully intend for those rules to be obeyed. And if those rules are deliberately broken, good parents dish out appropriate consequences.

God is our good and loving Heavenly Father. We were made in His image (Genesis 1:27), so we are like God in a lot of ways. And just like God establishes rules for His children, we make rules for our children. As God disciplines His children, we discipline our children. We want our children to obey, just like God wants His children to obey. As believers, we are God's children.

And if we defy His authority by disregarding His Word and disobeying His rules, we are behaving just as rebellious as a two-year-old who says, "NO!" or a teenager who stays out past curfew. And we will suffer the consequences of our rebellion.

Listen to what God says to Israel: **"Woe to the rebellious children ... that take counsel, but not of**

me; and that cover with a covering, but not of my spirit, that they may add sin to sin..."

Woe (misfortune or calamity):

- to the rebellious (those who defy authority) children...
- that take counsel (who seek advice), but not of me;
- and that cover with a covering (who hide themselves), but not of my spirit,
- that they may add sin to sin (who compounds one sin upon another).

Does this apply to His children today? Do we defy God's authority by neglecting His Word, whereby we disobey Him in everything we do? Do we follow ungodly advice and hide ourselves from the truth of God's Word while piling sin upon sin?

In Isaiah 65:2, God says, **"I have spread out my hands all the day unto a rebellious people, which walketh in a way that was not good, after their own thoughts..."**

To disobey God in anything makes you rebellious. And if you are living in rebellion, doing only what you think is right and not consulting God in anything, whichever way you go and whatever you do is not good. Let's remember how much God loves and cares for us. He wants us to walk in the right way and will guide us in that path if we let him.

It's well past time for God's children to put away rebellious thoughts and acts and learn to trust and obey their Savior – the One Who loved them so much that He sacrificed His life on Calvary for them.

The Commandments of God

Fear God and Keep His Commandments

> *"Ye shall diligently keep the commandments of the LORD your God, and his testimonies, and his statutes, which he hath commanded thee."*
>
> Deuteronomy 6:17

A command is an order given by someone who has authority, but a commandment is a "divine command." And who has more authority than God? No one.

Wait a minute! That's the Old Testament. That's the law. We're not under the law. We're under grace.

That's true. But does that mean that the Old Testament is invalid? No. Sixty-nine times in the New Testament, you will find the words, "it is written…" It's written where? The Old Testament.

Even Jesus quotes the Old Testament several times. Why would He quote the Old Testament if it no longer applied to New Testament believers?

Instead...

He reminds us of the importance of God's commandments when he says in John 13:34, **"A**

101

new commandment I give unto you, That ye love one another; as I have loved you, that ye also love one another."

In giving us a new commandment, Jesus didn't nullify the Old Testament commandments, but rather, He simply added one.

In Matthew 22:37-38, Jesus said, **"…Thou shalt love the Lord thy God with all thy heart, and with all thy soul, and with all thy mind. This is the first and great commandment."**

Jesus is quoting from Deuteronomy 6:5. Then He added, **"And the second is like unto it, Thou shalt love thy neighbour as thyself. On these two commandments hang all the law and the prophets."** (Matt. 22:39-40)

If believers strive to honor God by obeying these two commandments, Jesus wouldn't have to command us to love one another. We wouldn't steal from our neighbor or lie and gossip about him or cheat him (or her). We wouldn't misuse or abuse others in anyway. We'd be quick to forgive others as we desire God to forgive us.

That is what He means by **"On these two commandments hang all the law and the prophets."**

(Read the story of the good Samaritan in Luke 10:27-37. It gives Jesus' definition of 'neighbor.')

So, then, what does God want us to do?

"For this is the love of God, that we keep his commandments: and his commandments are not grievous." I John 5:3

"Let us hear the conclusion of the whole matter: Fear God, and keep his commandments: for this is the whole duty of man." Ecclesiastes 12:13

A Condition of Answered Prayer

"And whatsoever we ask, we receive of him, because we keep his commandments, and do those things that are pleasing in his sight.

And this is his commandment, That we should believe on the name of his Son Jesus Christ, and love one another, as he gave us commandment."

I John 3:22-23

I John 5:3 says, **"For this is the love of God, that we keep his commandments: and his commandments are not grievous."**

Grievous means to "cause intense mental anguish, deep remorse, or acute sorrow."

We serve a God of love. Because He's omniscient (knows everything) and full of wisdom, He never makes mistakes. Therefore, He knows what's best for us. So keeping His commandments would cause us no pain or regret. because God only wants the very best for His children.

So then, why don't we keep them?

Although we don't mind giving orders, we usually don't like taking them? Why is that? Because we want to make our own decisions, and we don't like someone else telling us what to do. Children rebel against their parents' authority. Wives resist submitting to their husbands. Employees don't appreciate their employers giving them instructions on their job. A lot of people break the law. And no one likes to obey God.

We want control – of our decisions, of our lives, of our destinies – and to obey someone else means that they are calling the shots. Therefore, we feel like they have the control. And we don't like it, not even if that someone is God.

But everybody has to answer to somebody. Do you expect your children to obey regardless of whether or not they like your rules? Of course, you do. Those rules are in place for a reason, even when your children don't recognize their value. And God is no different. Because He loves us, He wants us to do right, so He gave us some important commandments to honor and obey.

I John 3:22 says, **"And whatsoever we ask, we receive of him, because we keep his commandments, and do those things that are pleasing in his sight."**

It pleases God when we obey Him with a right attitude, so He delights in answering our prayers.

I John 3:23 says, **"And this is his commandment, That we should believe on the name of his Son Jesus**

Christ, and love one another, as he gave us commandment."

Those are two simple commandments: to believe on the name of God's Son, Jesus, and to love each other. If you do those two things, you will please God. And when you please God, He will hear your prayer.

Abiding in His Love

> *"And he that keepeth his commandments dwelleth in him, and he in him. And hereby we know that he abideth in us, by the Spirit which he hath given us."*
>
> I John 3:24

Jesus loves us whether or not we obey His Word.

However, in John 15:10 He said, **"If ye keep my commandments, ye shall abide in my love; even as I have kept my Father's commandments, and abide in his love."**

To abide means "to remain in one place or state; to continue." If we abide in Christ's love, we live our lives in a continual state of love, which is one of the nine-fold fruit of the Spirit (Galatians 5:22). We love God. We love our neighbors. We love our friends. And we even love our enemies.

Luke 6:27 says, **"But I say unto you which hear, Love your enemies, do good to them which hate you."**

That is also a commandment of God. And when we choose to honor God by obeying His Word and keeping His commandments, He allows us to abide in His love.

To dwell means "to live as a resident; to reside." To "dwell in him" and to allow Christ to dwell in us is to permeate our very existence with Christ; Everything in life revolves around our Savior. His Word. His commandments. His will.

In John 14:23, Jesus said, **"...If a man love me, he will keep my words: and my Father will love him, and we will come unto him, and make our abode with him."**

An abode is a dwelling place; a place where one resides. Is there anything greater than knowing that God Almighty, the Creator of all the universe, knows you personally and wants to reside with you?

Romans 5:5 says, **"And hope maketh not ashamed; because the love of God is shed abroad in our hearts by the Holy Ghost which is given unto us."**

Because of God's love, He has given His Spirit to His children that we might love others as He loves us. He has also given us commandments – divine rules – to live by. By obeying God's commandments, we show Him that we love Him.

I John 5:3 says, **"For this is the love of God, that we keep his commandments: and his commandments are not grievous."**

Grievous means to cause grief or suffering. God's commandments were not intended to bring us hardship but to develop godly character and make us more like Him. So those individuals who keep God's commandments dwell in Christ, and Christ dwells in them.

I John 4:13 says, **"Hereby know we that we dwell in him, and he in us, because he hath given us of his Spirit."**

The Great Commandment

"...Thou shalt love the Lord thy God with all thy heart, and with all thy soul, and with all thy mind.

This is the first and great commandment.

And the second is like unto it, Thou shalt love thy neighbour as thyself."

Matthew 22:37-39

We were created to love and worship God.

- God gives us life.
- God gives us love.
- God gives us His Son.
- God gives us salvation.
- God gives us His Word.
- God gives us His protection.
- God gives us His continual care.
- God gives us His commandments.

God gives and gives and gives again. He's faithful and kind and merciful and loving and full of goodness. He cannot lie, and He loves us far more than we love ourselves.

We, on the other hand, were sinners. We were full of pride and arrogance, often ungrateful, unforgiving, unkind, and unloving. Before we were saved, by nature, we displayed the traits contrary to those of God.

Yet, II Corinthians 5:17 says, **"Therefore if any man be in Christ, he is a new creature: old things are passed away; behold, all things are become new."**

When you got saved, God gave you a new nature in Christ. Now you have what it takes to be like Him: faithful, kind, merciful, forgiving, loving, honest...

And God wants us to be just like He is. That's why He's given us the two greatest commandments on Earth:

1. **"Love the Lord thy God with all thy heart, and with all thy soul, and with all thy mind."**

To love God that much means to take all your focus off of yourself and place it on Him; to let your life revolve around God and His Word, His will, His ways, His plans, His goodness; to obey God in such a way that you yield total control of your life to Him. Only then can you love God with all your heart, mind, and soul.

2. **"Love thy neighbour as thyself."**

Now to truly love your neighbor as yourself, you must have the heart of God. And that comes from obeying the Word of God. The more you obey God's Word, the less you focus on yourself (your wants, goals, and desires), and the more concern you show for the needs and cares of others.

If you will strive to obey these two great commandments, you will live a life of continual joy and peace through Christ Jesus your Savior.

Psalm 119:165 says, **"Great peace have they which love thy law: and nothing shall offend them."**

Isaiah 26:3 says, **"Thou wilt keep him in perfect peace, whose mind is stayed on thee: because he trusteth in thee."**

There is nothing in this world more precious than peace. And it's the natural reward of your obedience to God's commandments.

Respect God's Commandments

"Then shall I not be ashamed, when I have respect unto all thy commandments."

Psalm 119:6

According to the dictionary, the word shame means "a feeling of distress or humiliation caused by consciousness of the guilt or folly of oneself or an associate."

At one time or another we've all felt a sense of shame or embarrassment due to our own careless actions or those of someone else. Unfortunately, that feeling is all too often a part of life, and no one likes it. But while we have no guarantee that we (or someone we love) won't cause us shame, we have absolute certainty that God will never bring shame to us in any way. We can trust His Word completely.

- God's Word is absolute truth. It will never mislead you. (John 17:17)
- God's Word will lighten your path. It will not leave you in darkness. (Psalm 119:105)
- God's Word encourages, instructs, and guides you through life. You'll never be alone again. (Proverbs 3:5-6)

- God's Word transforms your life into one that pleases Him. It's trustworthy. (Romans 12:2)
- God's Word gives you peace and direction. You no longer have to fear the unknown. (Psalm 4:8)
- God's Word is pure, holy, and infallible. He makes no mistakes. (Psalm 12:6-7)

Honoring God's commandments will never bring us shame or cause embarrassment.

Psalm 78:7-8 says, **"That they might set their hope in God, and not forget the works of God, but keep his commandments: And might not be as their fathers, a stubborn and rebellious generation; a generation that set not their heart aright, and whose spirit was not stedfast with God."**

Is your spirit steadfast with God? Do you have respect for all His commandments?

To have respect unto all God's commandments means to regard them with deference, esteem, or honor. In other words, because we have high regard and great respect for His Word, we readily obey all God's commandments. But before we can obey them, we must first *know* them. Then you will strive to diligently learn them thoroughly...

- Personal Bible study – read, study, and meditate on God's Word daily.
- Regular attendance at a solid Gospel preaching, Bible believing church.
- Faithful Sunday school attendance.
- Prayer for wisdom and spiritual growth.
- Allowing the Holy Spirit to teach you.
- Most importantly, you must apply what you learn.

James 1:22 says, **"But be ye doers of the word, and not hearers only, deceiving your own selves."**

The wise fear the Lord. The wise have respect unto His commandments.

Give instruction to a wise man, and he will be yet wiser: teach a just man, and he will increase in learning. Proverbs 9:9

Proverbs 3:35 says, **"The wise shall inherit glory: but shame shall be the promotion of fools."**

The Fear of God

What Does it Mean to Fear the Lord?

"By mercy and truth iniquity is purged: and by the fear of the Lord men depart from evil."

Proverbs 16:6

What is the fear of the Lord? Are we supposed to be afraid of God? God is not a tyrant who gets pleasure out of frightening people.

Psalm 145:8 says, **"The LORD is gracious, and full of compassion; slow to anger, and of great mercy."**

I John 4:16 says, **"And we have known and believed the love that God hath to us. God is love; and he that dwelleth in love dwelleth in God, and God in him."**

As you can see, the Bible says that God is love. He's merciful and full of compassion toward us. So, then, what does the Bible mean when it tells us to fear the Lord?

- We need to reverence His Name. **"He sent redemption unto his people: he hath commanded his covenant for ever: holy and reverend is his name."** Psalm 111:9
- We need to recognize Him for who He is: the Creator of all living. **"For the LORD your God is God of gods, and Lord of lords, a great God, a mighty, and a terrible, which regardeth**

119

not persons, nor taketh reward:" Deuteronomy 10:17

- We need to recognize His awesome might. **"That all the people of the earth might know the hand of the LORD, that it is mighty: that ye might fear the LORD your God for ever."** Joshua 4:24

- We need to recognize His greatness. **"For the LORD is great, and greatly to be praised: he is to be feared above all gods. For all the gods of the nations are idols: but the LORD made the heavens."** Psalm 96:4-5

- We need to know that He has the power to cast mankind into an eternal hell. **"And fear not them which kill the body, but are not able to kill the soul: but rather fear him which is able to destroy both soul and body in hell."** Matthew 10:28

The Bible is very clear when it talks about the love, mercy, kindness, and compassion of God. But that doesn't mean that we should discount His justice and judgment and pending wrath. The same Bible that assures us of God's love and mercy, also warns us of His wrath and a coming judgment.

- Romans 1:18 **"For the wrath of God is revealed from heaven against all ungodliness and unrighteousness of men, who hold the truth in unrighteousness."**

- Psalm 7:11 **"God judgeth the righteous, and God is angry with the wicked every day."**
- Psalm 90:11 **"Who knoweth the power of thine anger? even according to thy fear, so is thy wrath."**
- I Peter 4:17-18 **"For the time is come that judgment must begin at the house of God: and if it first begin at us, what shall the end be of them that obey not the gospel of God? And if the righteous scarcely be saved, where shall the ungodly and the sinner appear?"**

To fear the Lord simply means that you have a healthy respect for His authority as Creator, a reverence for His holy Name, and a recognition of His holiness and awesome power. No person who experiences the fear of God Almighty as the Bible warns will reject His gift of salvation.

Do you know the Savior? If not, it is not too late. Ask God to give you a glimpse of His might and power. You will *never* forget it.

The Beginning of Wisdom

"The fear of the LORD is the beginning of wisdom: a good understanding have all they that do his commandments: his praise endureth for ever."

Psalm 111:10

Those with God's wisdom obey his commandments, which means that they have good understanding.

A good understanding of what?

A good understanding of God's commands (or His orders and instructions). It's impossible to obey a command that you do not understand. That good understanding accompanies wisdom, and the fear of the Lord is the beginning of wisdom.

And you'll discover that the fear of the Lord is the forerunner of all other blessings. It starts with wisdom and understanding.

Jesus will never leave you.

"Teaching them to observe all things whatsoever I have commanded you: and, lo, I am with you alway, even unto the end of the world. Amen." Matthew 28:20

Jesus is your friend.

"Ye are my friends, if ye do whatsoever I command you." John 15:14

Jesus loves you and reveals Himself to you.

"He that hath my commandments, and keepeth them, he it is that loveth me: and he that loveth me shall be loved of my Father, and I will love him, and will manifest myself to him." John 14:21

You will forever remain in His love.

"If ye keep my commandments, ye shall abide in my love; even as I have kept my Father's commandments, and abide in his love." John 15:10

You will enter the gates of Heaven.

"Blessed are they that do his commandments, that they may have right to the tree of life, and may enter in through the gates into the city." Revelation 22:14

I John 2:3 says, "And hereby we do know that we know him, if we keep his commandments."

According to the dictionary, the word wisdom means "good judgment and intelligence in knowing what is right, good, and true." So for us to even begin to understand what is right, good, and true, we must fear the LORD.

For **"the fear of the LORD is the beginning of wisdom..."**

To fear the LORD means to reverence His Name and to recognize Him for who He is: the Creator of all living, our great and mighty God, to give Him the respect and honor due Him.

What is right, good, and true?

- God is good and right, and He'll teach you as you go through life. **"Good and upright is the LORD: therefore will he teach sinners in the way."** Psalm 25:8
- God's judgments are true. **"The fear of the LORD is clean, enduring for ever: the judgments of the LORD are true and righteous altogether."** Psalm 19:9
- Jesus is the Truth. Jesus said, **"...I am the way, the truth, and the life: no man cometh unto the Father, but by me."** John 14:6
- The Bible is Truth: **"Sanctify them through thy truth: thy word is truth."** John 17:17

And while God is good and right, His judgments are true, His Son is Truth, and His Word is Truth.

Proverbs 3:7 says, **"Be not wise in thine own eyes: fear the LORD, and depart from evil."**

In other words, let go of your worldly wisdom and fear the Lord. Then He'll give you the wisdom to depart from evil.

Because **"The fear of the LORD is the beginning of wisdom."** (Psalm 111:10)

The Beginning of Knowledge

> *"The fear of the LORD is the beginning of knowledge: but fools despise wisdom and instruction."*
>
> Proverbs 1:7

Our country revolves around knowledge. That's why we put such a high priority on a good education, and we would agree that **"fools despise wisdom and instruction."** But without God, there is no knowledge.

I Samuel 2:3 says, **"...for the LORD is a God of knowledge, and by him actions are weighed."** All knowledge comes from God, and **"The fear of the LORD is the beginning of knowledge..."**

I Timothy 2:4 says, **"Who will have all men to be saved, and to come unto the knowledge of the truth."**

God wants us to be saved and come to the knowledge of the truth. Truth is not relative; it's absolute. The dictionary defines knowledge as an "awareness or familiarity gained by experience."

Yet, II Timothy 3:7 says, **"Ever learning, and never able to come to the knowledge of the truth."**

Knowledge apart from truth is worthless.

Jesus said in John 14:6, **"... I am the truth ..."** He also said in John 17:17, **"... thy word is truth."** Without the fear of the LORD in our lives, we are devoid of truth.

The fear of the LORD brings us a healthy respect and reverence for God, our Creator; Jesus, His Son; the Holy Spirit, our Comforter; and God's Word, the Holy Bible. If we lack reverence for even One in the Holy Trinity or for God's Word, we do not fear the LORD, in which case, we have no knowledge of the Truth.

Proverbs 1:29 says, **"For that they hated knowledge, and did not choose the fear of the LORD:"**

Living in a society that almost worships knowledge and education, the Bible tells us where to find what we're looking for.

Proverbs 2:3-6 says, **"Yea, if thou criest after knowledge, and liftest up thy voice for understanding; If thou seekest her as silver, and searchest for her as for hid treasures; Then shalt thou understand the fear of the LORD, and find the knowledge of God. For the LORD giveth wisdom: out of his mouth cometh knowledge and understanding."**

II Corinthians 4:6 says, **"For God, who commanded the light to shine out of darkness, hath shined in our hearts, to give the light of the knowledge of the glory of God in the face of Jesus Christ."**

Psalm 111:10 says, **"The fear of the LORD is the beginning of wisdom: a good understanding have all they that do his commandments: his praise endureth for ever."**

Proverbs 1:7 says, **"The fear of the LORD is the beginning of knowledge: but fools despise wisdom and instruction."**

Our only source of knowledge and wisdom is God Almighty. And it starts with **"the fear of the LORD."**

Depart from Evil

"He will fulfil the desire of them that fear him: he also will hear their cry, and will save them."

Psalm 145:19

For those who love and fear the Lord, He is always nearby, and He will fulfill their desire. Verse 20 tells us what desire He will fulfill. **"The LORD preserveth all them that love him: but all the wicked will he destroy."**

Everyone desires protection, and God promises to preserve the righteous. In other words, He will take care of those who love and fear Him.

Matthew 6:31 & 33 says, **"Therefore take no thought, saying, What shall we eat? or, What shall we drink? or, Wherewithal shall we be clothed? ... But seek ye first the kingdom of God, and his righteousness; and all these things shall be added unto you."**

If we strive to please the Lord in all we do – to love, honor, and obey Him; to live righteously; to put Him first in every area of our lives – He'll automatically fulfill our natural desire to have our physical needs met. And with confidence we can

129

cast all our cares upon Him because He will take care of them. (I Peter 5:7)

So what exactly does it mean to fear the Lord? Does God expect us to cower in His holy presence? Does He delight in terrorizing us like an abusive parent beats a child into submission? No!

II Timothy 1:7 says, **"For God hath not given us the spirit of fear; but of power, and of love, and of a sound mind."**

We serve a God of love and mercy who has given us a sound mind to make godly decisions and His power to see them through. So fearing God is not an emotion. *It's an action!*

According to Scripture, here's the definition of fearing the Lord: **"The fear of the LORD is to hate evil: pride, and arrogancy, and the evil way, and the froward mouth, do I hate."** (Proverbs 8:13)

The colon after evil means that the Bible is now defining evil. Evil is defined as pride, arrogance, the evil way (anything ungodly), and a perverse mouth.

Wow! That means the fear of the Lord and humility go hand-in-hand.

II Chronicles 19:7 says, **"Wherefore now let the fear of the LORD be upon you; take heed and do it: for**

there is no iniquity with the LORD our God, nor respect of persons, nor taking of gifts."

We serve a holy God who detests sin in any form. He plays no favorites, and He takes no bribes. If we fear the Lord, we'll also hate sin. *All sin!* Even our own. And that hatred for sin will cause us to repent.

Proverbs 3:7 says, **"Be not wise in thine own eyes: fear the LORD, and depart from evil."**

If you do, He promises to hear your cry for help and save you from destruction.

Pleasing God

> **"The LORD taketh pleasure in them that fear him, in those that hope in his mercy."**
>
> Psalm 147:11

Psalm 103:13 says, **"Like as a father pitieth his children, so the LORD pitieth them that fear him."**

According to the dictionary, pity means "sorrow or compassion aroused by another's condition." God is more than aroused by our hopeless condition. He responds to those who recognize their sinful state and turn to Him for mercy.

- He gives mercy to those who fear Him. **"And his mercy is on them that fear him from generation to generation."** Luke 1:50
- He shows them His goodness. **"Oh how great is thy goodness, which thou hast laid up for them that fear thee; which thou hast wrought for them that trust in thee before the sons of men!"** Psalm 31:19
- He accepts the righteous from every nation. **"But in every nation he that feareth him, and worketh righteousness, is accepted with him."** Acts 10:35

Without the fear of the Lord, we have no way to discern between good and evil, no wisdom, no knowledge, no understanding.

Proverbs 1:7 says, **"The fear of the LORD is the beginning of knowledge: but fools despise wisdom and instruction."**

Proverbs 3:7 says, **"Be not wise in thine own eyes: fear the LORD, and depart from evil."**

Proverbs 9:10 says, **"The fear of the LORD is the beginning of wisdom: and the knowledge of the holy is understanding."**

What does it mean to "fear the Lord?" It means to recognize Him for Who He is.

- Almighty God
- The Creator of Heaven and Earth and all that lives within them
- The Alpha and the Omega, the Beginning and the End
- The King Eternal
- All wise, all knowing, all present, and all powerful.

The Great I AM

You must reverence and praise His holy Name because of Who He Is - our Almighty Creator and merciful Savior.

Deuteronomy 10:12-13 says, **"And now, Israel, what doth the LORD thy God require of thee, but to fear the LORD thy God, to walk in all his ways, and to love him, and to serve the LORD thy God with all thy heart and with all thy soul, To keep the commandments of the LORD, and his statutes, which I command thee this day for thy good?"**

Jesus called this the first and great commandment. If we fear God in this way, then He will take delight in us, too.

Judgment's Coming

> *"And fear not them which kill the body, but are not able to kill the soul: but rather fear him which is able to destroy both soul and body in hell."*
>
> Matthew 10:28

II Peter 3:9 says, **"The Lord is not slack concerning his promise, as some men count slackness; but is longsuffering to us-ward, not willing that any should perish, but that all should come to repentance."**

We serve a kind and loving God who wishes that no one should go to hell. However, on Judgment Day, Jesus will say to those who have rejected Him, **"...Depart from me, ye cursed, into everlasting fire, prepared for the devil and his angels."** (Matthew 25:41)

Hell was never intended for mankind. God doesn't want us to go there. That's why He provided for our salvation.

Titus 1:2 says, **"In hope of eternal life, which God, that cannot lie, promised before the world began."**

And Hebrews 2:3 says, **"How shall we escape, if we neglect so great salvation; which at the first began to be spoken by the Lord, and was confirmed unto us by them that heard him."**

I John 4:16 says, **"And we have known and believed the love that God hath to us. God is love; and he that dwelleth in love dwelleth in God, and God in him."**

If the Bible affirms that God is love, why does Matthew 10:28 tell us to **"fear him which is able to destroy both soul and body in hell."** We know that verse is referring to God.

I John 4:17-18 says, **"Herein is our love made perfect, that we may have boldness in the day of judgment: because as he is, so are we in this world. There is no fear in love; but perfect love casteth out fear: because fear hath torment. He that feareth is not made perfect in love."**

It's because of God's love for us that He provided a way of escape from hell, but it's because of our love for God that we no longer have to fear the White Throne Judgment.

So then, if we are made perfect in love and perfect love casts out fear, what does the Bible mean when it instructs us to fear God? God doesn't expect us to fear Him like we would a big bully who's threatened to beat us up. To fear God means to respect Him for Who He is and what He's capable of doing; to hold Him in reverential awe.

Hebrews 12:28 says, **"Wherefore we receiving a kingdom which cannot be moved, let us have grace,**

whereby we may serve God acceptably with reverence and godly fear."

God is love, but He is also just. And one day everyone will face Him in judgment.

The Goodness
of God

With Jesus as our Guide - A Testimony

When determination strikes a child of God, sometimes all common sense (by worldly standards) is put on hold, especially when it involves a responsibility we take seriously.

You have only one thing on your mind and that's accomplishing your goal. When that happens, God may intervene (before we hurt ourselves), but sometimes He chooses to overshadow us with His protection and sees us through the danger.

When Floyd transferred from RAF (Royal Air Force) Alconbury, England to Moody Air Force Base in Georgia, the military transported our family back to the States. They flew us into New Jersey and we had about a week before Floyd had to report for duty at Moody AFB.

The military would have arranged our transportation all the way to our new base, but Floyd wasn't ready to head for Georgia. He wanted to run up to Michigan and pick up his Ford super cab pickup truck from a friend. Then we drove on to northern Wisconsin to collect his fifth-wheel trailer from his mom and dad.

Hooking the camper to the back of his pickup, we headed for our new base down south.

Military service members in transit are required to be at their assigned duty sections by a certain day and time, or they are considered AWOL (Absent With Out Leave), and they can get in serious trouble.

Well, we had just enough time to pick up his truck and trailer before heading down to Valdosta, Georgia. With time a factor, our little family turned south. Floyd's truck had bench seats, so our 20-month old son was strapped in between us.

Listening to the radio, we knew that we were going to cross paths with a blizzard, so it was a race against time. If that blizzard hit us, we'd get stranded and Floyd wouldn't report for duty at Moody on time. He'd be AWOL. And the military doesn't make exceptions due to circumstances, especially when we had the option to be transported all the way to our base.

As we neared Chicago, between the wind, heavy snowfall, and drifting snow, travel became almost impossible.

I tuned the radio into a Chicago station for weather updates and road closings. The snowfall was so heavy that drifting snow caused them to close the southbound freeway. Forced to exit the freeway in Chicago, we pulled into a truck stop.

Floyd said, "If anyone knows how to get through this, it'll be a trucker." So he sent me in to ask them which roads would take us south.

But the truckers didn't see a way. They told me, "You won't get through. Find a motel and ride out the storm. It'll probably be three or four days before you can get out."

We didn't have three or four days, so I bought a map of the Chicago area and we found a street heading south. Then we trusted Jesus to guide us through.

It was like trying to get through a maze. We drove a couple miles before we ran into another road closure and had to exit. For a couple of hours, we zigzagged through Chicago streets in search of an open southbound road, and we stayed on it until it closed, all the while listening to the radio.

They closed road after road right in front of us, each time forcing us to turn onto an east or westbound road.

Finally, we found a two-lane, southbound road that was still open. The snow drifting on that road was so bad that there was no more than a two-foot gap down the center of the road that was free of snow at any given time, and some of the drifts completely covered the road.

With no traffic due to the blizzard and drifting snow making it difficult to get through, Floyd drove down the middle of the road where the snow was the shallowest. Even then, the snow got so deep in spots that his pickup truck got stuck, but the weight of his fifth wheeler shoved us through, spraying snow out either direction. That happened time and time again. As we passed through intersections, I read the street signs of the cross streets.

Due to severe snow drifting, they again closed the road we were on. Only this time, as we listened to the radio, we heard that the road had been closed *behind us*. They closed that road at one intersection after another shortly after we had crossed it. We practically flew down that road to get out of Chicago before they closed the road in front of us.

As we hit each deep snowdrift in the road, the truck jerked to a stop and the trailer shoved it through. And behind us were a whole line of cars, following in our tracks as Floyd's truck and trailer blazed a trail through each snowdrift. (That's how we're to be as Christians, leading others to Christ, blazing a trail through life's deep snow drifts for others to follow.)

That little two-lane road took us right back to the Interstate. But when we finally reached the on-ramp, there sat a police car, blocking the entrance.

We thought, *Oh, no.*

Pulling alongside the patrol car, Floyd rolled down his window. The officer said, "Which way are you folks headed?" Floyd replied, "South." The officer said, "Have a nice trip."

It took us eight hours to go 100 miles, but with God's help, we got through. With Jesus as our guide, and determination on our side, Floyd reported to Moody AFB on time.

God's Continual Blessings

"Oh that men would praise the LORD for his goodness, and for his wonderful works to the children of men!"

Psalm 107:8

Why don't we praise God for his goodness and the wonderful things that He does for us each and every day? There are two reasons.

The first and most likely reason is that we don't recognize God's goodness and the things He does for us each day. Maybe we even attribute God's blessings to our own hard work and diligence

The second reason is that we don't appreciate what He does for us because we feel it's our right to have those good things.

I've been told on several different occasions, *"God hasn't given me anything! I work for everything I have."*

The individual who holds this view fails to recognize everything that God has blessed them with, such as health, a job, and a healthy family.

- One sick child can deplete your entire savings due to insurmountable medical bills.

- A house fire, flood, tornado, or hurricane can wipe out everything you've worked for, in addition to taking your precious loved one.
- A car accident can leave you permanently disabled and unable to work.

If you've never been touched by one of these tragedies, you've been tremendously blessed by God. But if you have experienced a financial or personal loss due to anything that's beyond your control, be aware that Psalm 52:1 says, **"...the goodness of God endureth continually."**

God's goodness didn't stop just because of a tragedy in your family. So how does God display His goodness toward us?

Jesus gives us rest.

"Come unto me, all ye that labour and are heavy laden, and I will give you rest." Matthew 11:28

Jesus hears us when we pray.

"And I say unto you, Ask, and it shall be given you; seek, and ye shall find; knock, and it shall be opened unto you. For every one that asketh receiveth; and he that seeketh findeth; and to him that knocketh it shall be opened." Luke 11:9-10

Jesus gives us peace.

"Peace I leave with you, my peace I give unto you: not as the world giveth, give I unto you. Let not your heart be troubled, neither let it be afraid." John 14:27

Jesus sends us the Comforter

"Nevertheless I tell you the truth; It is expedient for you that I go away: for if I go not away, the Comforter will not come unto you; but if I depart, I will send him unto you." John 16:7

Jesus gives us truth.

"Sanctify them through thy truth: thy word is truth." John 17:17

Jesus gives us safety.

"I will both lay me down in peace, and sleep: for thou, LORD, only makest me dwell in safety." Psalm 4:8

Jesus gives us the desires of our hearts.

"Delight thyself also in the LORD; and he shall give thee the desires of thine heart." Psalm 37:4

Jesus gives us guidance.

"Trust in the LORD with all thine heart; and lean not unto thine own understanding. In all thy ways acknowledge him, and he shall direct thy paths."
Proverbs 3:5-6

Jesus gives us loving discipline.

"For whom the Lord loveth he chasteneth, and scourgeth every son whom he receiveth. If ye endure chastening, God dealeth with you as with sons; for what son is he whom the father chasteneth not?"
Hebrews 12:6-7

Jesus gave Himself.

"Herein is love, not that we loved God, but that he loved us, and sent his Son to be the propitiation for our sins." I John 4:10

Jesus offers us eternal life.

"For the wages of sin is death; but the gift of God is eternal life through Jesus Christ our Lord."
Romans 6:23

Jesus provides our needs.

"But my God shall supply all your need according to his riches in glory by Christ Jesus." Philippians 4:19

Jesus gives us His mercy.

"Not by works of righteousness which we have done, but according to his mercy he saved us, by the washing of regeneration, and renewing of the Holy Ghost." Titus 3:5

Exodus 34:6-7 says, **"And the LORD passed by before him** [Moses]**, and proclaimed, The LORD, The LORD God, merciful and gracious, longsuffering, and abundant in goodness and truth, Keeping mercy for thousands, forgiving iniquity and transgression and sin...."**

As you can see, God's blessings are innumerable and without end. What has God done for you today? Have you thanked Him?

The Lord is Good

> *"The LORD is good, a strong hold in the day of trouble; and he knoweth them that trust in him."*
>
> Nahum 1:7

There are three valuable truths about God Almighty that we can glean from this verse.

The Lord is good.

Everything He does is good. Everything He says is good. Therefore, His guidance and direction are good. They're right. They're always what we need to hear, regardless of what we want to hear. That means we can always trust Him.

He's a stronghold in the day of trouble.

A stronghold is a fortress or a source of refuge. God is a place where we can run for protection during times of trouble. He'll safeguard us. He knows those who trust in Him.

He personally knows each and every one who has placed their trust in Him.

The Lord is good to everyone, whether or not they deserve it.

Matthew 5:45 says, **"That ye may be the children of your Father which is in heaven: for he maketh his sun to rise on the evil and on the good, and sendeth rain on the just and on the unjust."**

There are some blessings that God grants to everyone. But He's not a stronghold to everyone; only to those who trust in Him. Because only those who trust in Him will run to Him in times of trouble.

And He knows those who trust in Him.

God is Good to Those Who Fear Him

"Oh how great is thy goodness, which thou hast laid up for them that fear thee; which thou hast wrought for them that trust in thee before the sons of men!"

Psalm 31:19

God's goodness is greater than we can begin to comprehend. Trying to understand God's goodness is like trying to understand how hot the sun is or the vastness of outer space. We know the sun is hot and we recognize that space is big, even though our tools of measurement are limited. Likewise, we know that God is good. And His goodness has been laid up for those who fear Him – who recognize his awesome might and power; and God has prepared incredibly good things for those who trust in Him.

God bestows abundant goodness on those who fear Him. But what exactly does it mean "to fear the Lord?" That means to recognize Jesus for Who He truly is – God Almighty, the all-knowing and all-powerful Creator of the universe. And with that recognition, we should honor Him with the esteem and respect that He deserves as our Creator.

God's Goodness on Those Who Fear Him.

Joshua 4:24 says, **"That all the people of the earth might know the hand of the LORD, that it is mighty: that ye might fear the LORD your God for ever."**

God wants you to know that His hand is mighty.

Proverbs 3:7 says, **"Be not wise in thine own eyes: fear the LORD, and depart from evil."**

To fear the Lord, you must first recognize who He is; and then you will better understand your shortcomings and failures. Only then will you **"be not wise in thine own eyes … and depart from evil."**

God's Goodness on Those who Trust Him.

Psalm 125:1 says, **"They that trust in the LORD shall be as mount Zion, which cannot be removed, but abideth for ever."**

The goodness of God keeps you solid as a mountain.

Isaiah 26:4 says, **"Trust ye in the LORD for ever: for in the LORD JEHOVAH is everlasting strength."**

The goodness of God provides you with everlasting strength.

Psalm 34:8 says, **"O taste and see that the LORD is good: blessed is the man that trusteth in him."**

The goodness of God blesses the person who trusts in Him.

Do you recognize the goodness of God? His goodness is in everything you do and everywhere you go.

God's Promise to Those Who Love Him

"And we know that all things work together for good to them that love God, to them who are the called according to his purpose."

Romans 8:28

We like living in comfort.

- Having a good job which provides enough money, medical insurance, and a retirement income
- Respectful and responsible children
- A nice home and a good-running car
- Limited stress
- A healthy family

The list is endless. But those things are often in short supply, and our comfort can easily get chipped away by an accident or tragedy, a layoff or extended hospital stay, rebellious children or a natural disaster that wipes out everything we own.

When those things come your way, and they will, how do you respond? What do you do? Where do you turn?

Remember that **"...all things work together for good to them that love God, to them who are the called according to his purpose."**

- This verse doesn't promise that you won't lose your job, but that God will work it out for your good.
- This verse doesn't promise that you won't have a car accident, but that God will work it out for your good.
- This verse doesn't promise that you won't suffer the loss of a child or spouse, but that God will work it out for your good.
- This verse doesn't promise that you won't lose your home to a flood or fire, but that God will work it out for your good.
- This verse doesn't promise that you or a well-loved family member won't be diagnosed with cancer, but that God will work it out for your good.

Regardless of the challenge you're facing right now, remember that God can and will work it out for your good if you **"are the called according to his purpose."**

Now, what exactly does that mean?

That means that you are doing everything you know God would have you to do. We can't live foolishly and expect God to work out our stupidity for our good. That's why that verse adds the condition **"...to them who are the called according to his purpose."**

It's not God's purpose for you to drink and drive or take illegal drugs or engage in any type of ungodly activities. God never promises to work out for good the problems that arise due to choices that we make while living outside of a holy lifestyle, and we're all called to live a holy lifestyle.

What challenges are you facing today? Are you living a life **"according to His purpose?"**

The Grace of
God

Received by Adoption

"And the LORD...proclaimed, The LORD, The LORD God, merciful and gracious, longsuffering, and abundant in goodness and truth,

Keeping mercy for thousands, forgiving iniquity and transgression and sin, and that will by no means clear the guilty..."

Exodus 34:6-7

God declares Himself to be gracious. What does "gracious" mean? According to the dictionary, it means gentle, kind, and merciful, but God says that He is also patient, good, forgiving, and truthful. It's because of these attributes that He extends unto us His grace.

Grace means God's unmerited (or unearned) favor. And there's absolutely nothing we can do to earn it or deserve it because of our sinful nature or flesh. At our very best, we are not good enough to compare to the King of Glory and His righteousness.

We may think we can earn it or that we're good enough to deserve it. That only shows God how little we know about His righteousness and standards of perfection.

Let's compare a multi-billionaire to an orphaned child who's been living on the streets fending for herself. When she comes to him, she's barefoot, incredibly dirty, dressed in tattered clothes, covered in sores and lice with no means to clean herself up before she approaches him.

But he's kind and good and merciful, and he takes that little child into his home. He adopts her, accepting her just like she is. Then she's bathed and de-liced. He gives her brand new clothes and shoes. He takes her to the doctor where she receives the best medical care and puts her in a school where she'll receive the very best education.

She now has a home and can call him "Daddy."

He loves her and cares for her, and from now on, he will provide all her needs. She'll never be in want again. In addition, she is now his heir.

What did this child do to earn her position as his daughter? Nothing.

What did she do to deserve his mercy and kindness? Nothing.

She had nothing to offer, nothing to give him that he could possibly want in exchange for his favor on her wretched young life. And that's how we come to Jesus: wretched and dirty.

Isaiah 64:6 says, **"But we are all as an unclean thing, and all our righteousnesses are as filthy rags; and we**

all do fade as a leaf; and our iniquities, like the wind, have taken us away."

You have nothing to offer God in exchange for His mercy and kindness. Absolutely nothing! Despite your miserable condition, God adopts you into his family, accepting you just as you are. *He* cleans you up and clothes you with His righteousness.

Revelation 1:5 says, **"And from Jesus Christ, who is the faithful witness, and the first begotten of the dead, and the prince of the kings of the earth. Unto him that loved us, and washed us from our sins in his own blood."**

He provides you with the best possible education by teaching you Himself.

John 16:13 says, **"Howbeit when he, the Spirit of truth, is come, he will guide you into all truth: for he shall not speak of himself; but whatsoever he shall hear, that shall he speak: and he will shew you things to come."**

What did you do to deserve that? Nothing. What did you do to earn it? Nothing. You enjoy the benefits and privileges of being adopted into God's family despite how unworthy you were when you came to Him.

That's the grace of God.

God Gives Grace and Glory

> *"For the LORD God is a sun and shield: the LORD will give grace and glory: no good thing will he withhold from them that walk uprightly."*
>
> Psalm 84:11

All good things come from God.

James 1:17 says, **"Every good gift and every perfect gift is from above, and cometh down from the Father of lights, with whom is no variableness, neither shadow of turning."**

The Lord provides His children with light and warmth just like the sun, and protects us from danger like a shield. He desires that we live righteously, and if we do, he promises to bless us with his favor (grace) and honor (glory).

And as Psalm 84:11 says, **"For the LORD God is a sun and shield...no good thing will he withhold from them that walk uprightly."**

God is a bright light in a dark world and as a shield, He protects us.

"... the LORD will give grace ..."

He will bestow upon us gifts and kindness that we haven't earned or deserved. (That's called grace.)

James 4:6 says, **"But he giveth more grace. Wherefore he saith, God resisteth the proud, but giveth grace unto the humble."**

If God only gives grace to the humble, then this verse applies only to the humble. And with grace, He will also give glory.

"...And glory..."

Glory means "honor." And God only honors the humble. For it's only the humble who honor Him.

In I Samuel 2:30, God says, **"... them that honour me I will honour, and they that despise me shall be lightly esteemed."**

So how do the humble honor God? Not only by their words, but also by their lives.

In Mark 7:6, Jesus said, **"... Well hath Esaias prophesied of you hypocrites, as it is written, This people honoureth me with their lips, but their heart is far from me."** (Isaiah 29:13)

"...No good thing will he withhold from them that walk uprightly."

Uprightly means "righteously, in a way that pleases God."

Only the humble can walk uprightly because the opposite of humility is pride, and pride is a sin. To hang onto your pride is to reject humility, which means that you're trusting in yourself and not

God. But those who humble themselves before God and honor Him in all they do by walking uprightly, He will give them grace and glory, and He will not withhold any good thing from them.

We are Saved by God's Grace

> *"For by grace are ye saved through faith; and that not of yourselves: it is the gift of God: Not of works, lest any man should boast."*
>
> Ephesians 2:8-9

The word grace means unearned favor. Therefore, to be saved by the grace of God means that salvation is given to you free and clear. You can't earn it; nor do you deserve it. But there is one thing you must do to benefit from it: You must receive it by faith. Salvation is a gift of God, bestowed on mankind through His grace. But that's not the only thing God's grace gives us.

Psalm 84:11 says, **"For the LORD God is a sun and shield: the LORD will give grace and glory: no good thing will he withhold from them that walk uprightly."**

Because of God's grace, the righteous are showered with His everlasting goodness and mercy. God favors His obedient children with good things. And when we experience God's continual blessings in our lives, we're experiencing His grace because we don't deserve any of His goodness.

II Corinthians 12:9 says, **"And he said unto me, My grace is sufficient for thee: for my strength is made perfect in weakness. Most gladly therefore will I**

rather glory in my infirmities, that the power of Christ may rest upon me."

God's grace is displayed through His power. When we are fainthearted and weak, Christ is then able to empower us with His strength and wisdom and guidance. Your weakness becomes God's strength through His grace and power.

All God's children understand salvation by grace through faith. (If they don't, then they're not really God's children.)

- By grace – we don't deserve salvation; nor could we ever attain to God's holy standards by our own merits. (Romans 3:10-12, 23)
- Through faith – we come to God just as we are, trusting Him to save us. (Romans 6:23; Ephesians 2:8-9)

Yet, although God's children trust His grace to save them, a lot of them reject His grace when it comes to keeping them.

"Not of yourselves" and **"not of works"** are very clear. No one can earn his way to Heaven, and anyone who believes that they can, are not saved because they're not trusting in God's saving grace, but rather their own righteousness. If there is nothing we can do to earn our salvation, then how is it that so many of God's children believe they must work in order to keep their salvation?

The Grace of God

I Peter 1:5 says, **"Who are kept by the power of God through faith unto salvation ready to be revealed in the last time."**

This is referring to believers. Ephesians 2:8 says that we're saved by grace through faith; then I Peter 1:5 says that we're kept by the power of God through faith.

"Now to him that worketh is the reward not reckoned of grace, but of debt." Romans 4:4

Our sin debt is too big to ever be paid. It's like owing someone a hundred trillion dollars. You could never pay it off. But when that person releases you from your financial obligation and stamps on your bill "Paid in Full," you are now free from your debt.

Then Romans 4:5 says, **"But to him that worketh not, but believeth on him that justifieth the ungodly, his faith is counted for righteousness."**

You see, it's by God's grace that we're saved, kept, blessed, strengthened, empowered, indwelt ...

"And if by grace, then is it no more of works: otherwise grace is no more grace ..." Romans 11:6

In other words, if the grace of God saves us and keeps us, then our works don't do anything to help us get saved, but if works could save, then we're not really saved by grace at all.

We are Taught by God's Grace

> *"For the grace of God that bringeth salvation hath appeared to all men,*
>
> *Teaching us that, denying ungodliness and worldly lusts, we should live soberly, righteously, and godly, in this present world;"*
>
> Titus 2:11-12

We have heard that grace is the unmerited favor of God. But what exactly does that mean? A merit is "something that entitles one to reward or gratitude." That means you've earned it. You cannot earn God's grace, otherwise, it wouldn't be grace. Grace is unmerited, which means that we're not entitled to it.

If we can't earn God's grace, and we're not entitled to it, how do we get it?

God freely gives it to those who love and obey Him.

Psalm 84:11 says, **"For the LORD God is a sun and shield: the LORD will give grace and glory: no good thing will he withhold from them that walk uprightly."**

God bestows His favor on all those who please Him. He gives grace and glory, and that means he will not withhold any good thing from those who live righteously.

But best of all, God's grace brings salvation to all mankind. That means salvation is available to everyone, but only through God's grace.

Ephesians 2:8-9 says, **"For by grace are ye saved through faith; and that not of yourselves: it is the gift of God: Not of works, lest any man should boast."**

We only have redemption through the blood of Christ **"the forgiveness of sins, according to the riches of his grace"** (Ephesians 1:7)

The grace of God is not only necessary for salvation, but also for spiritual maturity and growth.

The Lord gives grace. But what does His grace do?

- Grace brings salvation. (Titus 2:11)
- Grace teaches you to deny ungodliness and worldly lusts. (Titus 2:11-12)
- Grace teaches you to live soberly, righteously, and godly in this present world. (Titus 2:11-12
- Grace forgives sin. (Ephesians 1:7)

Also, God's grace is rich toward you in kindness through Christ (Ephesians 2:7), with faith and love (I Timothy 1:14), in your humility (James 4:6), and the grace of God empowers you for Christ (II Corinthians 12:9).

If you allow God's grace to permeate every area of your life, then you...

"...should live soberly, righteously, and godly, in this present world,"

In which case you will find yourself...

"Looking for that blessed hope, and the glorious appearing of the great God and our Saviour Jesus Christ; Who gave himself for us, that he might redeem us from all iniquity, and purify unto himself a peculiar people, zealous of good works." Titus 2:13-14

The "I AMs" of Christ

I AM the Great I AM

"Your father Abraham rejoiced to see my day: and he saw it, and was glad.

Then said the Jews unto him, Thou art not yet fifty years old, and hast thou seen Abraham?

Jesus said unto them, Verily, verily, I say unto you, Before Abraham was, I am."

John 8:56-58

A couple years after I got saved, someone told me that nowhere in Scripture did Jesus ever claim to be God. Of course, I was still a babe in Christ and hadn't read enough Scripture to know how to refute her statement. I knew she was wrong, so she never caused me to doubt. I just didn't know where to find a verse where Jesus said, "I am God."

But here in John 8:58, Jesus claims to be God when He says **"Before Abraham was, I am."** To put it in our modern day vernacular, Jesus meant, "Before Abraham was born, I existed."

In Exodus 3:14, **"... God said unto Moses, I AM THAT I AM: and he said, Thus shalt thou say unto the children of Israel, I AM hath sent me unto you."**

So when Jesus used God's title "I AM," He was saying, "I am the Eternal One. I am God." The

Jews knew what He was saying, and they were ready to stone Him for blasphemy.

Then in chapter ten, Jesus said, **"I and my Father are one."** (John 10:30) And once again, the Jews were ready to stone Him. They told Jesus in verse 33, **"For a good work we stone thee not; but for blasphemy; and because that thou, being a man, makest thyself God."**

The Jews heard what He said, and they knew exactly what He meant.

Colossians 1:15-16 tells us that Jesus is the Creator.

"Who is the image of the invisible God, the firstborn of every creature (That's Jesus – the image of God)**: For by him were all things created, that are in heaven, and that are in earth, visible and invisible, whether they be thrones, or dominions, or principalities, or powers: all things were created by him, and for him."** (Jesus created everything!)

And John 1:10 says, **"He was in the world, and the world was made by him, and the world knew him not."**

So God, the Creator of the universe, came into this world like any ordinary baby, grew up like an average child, and the world didn't even know it.

As the angel Gabriel told Mary in Luke 1:37 **"For with God nothing shall be impossible."**

And God Himself said to Jeremiah **"Behold, I am the LORD, the God of all flesh: is there any thing too hard for me?"** Jeremiah 32:27

The answer, of course, is no. Nothing is too hard for God.

Consider the greatest salvation verse known to mankind, John 3:16, which says **"For God so loved the world, that he gave his only begotten Son, that whosoever believeth in him should not perish, but have everlasting life."**

Every believer knows that Jesus died for our sins, yet I John 3:16 says that *God* died for us.

"Hereby perceive we the love of God, because he laid down his life for us: and we ought to lay down our lives for the brethren." I John 3:16

Jesus is God in the flesh, our Creator, our Savior, and the Great I AM. He said so Himself.

I AM the Son of God

"And the angel answered and said unto her, The Holy Ghost shall come upon thee, and the power of the Highest shall overshadow thee: therefore also that holy thing which shall be born of thee shall be called the Son of God."

Luke 1:35

According to Scriptures, **"a virgin shall conceive and bear a son"** (Isaiah 7:14; Luke 1:26-27) **"and shalt call His name Jesus"** (Luke 1:30-31). **"He shall be great, and shall be called the Son of the Highest..."** (Verse 32)

Who is the Highest? God Almighty. So if Jesus is the Son of the Highest, He is the Son of God. Yet, most people don't like hearing that and simply refuse to believe it.

People Freely Talk About God, but They Don't Like Jesus

Unfortunately, no one is able to get to God without going through Jesus.

Jesus said in John 14:6 **"...I am the way, the truth, and the life: no man cometh unto the Father, but by me."**

I John 2:23 says, **"Whosoever denieth the Son, the same hath not the Father: (but) he that acknowledgeth the Son hath the Father also."**

Jesus said, "I am the Son of God."

"Therefore the Jews sought the more to kill him, because he not only had broken the sabbath, but said also that God was his Father, making himself equal with God." (John 5:18)

If Jesus said that God was His Father, that means He claimed to be the Son of God.

Jesus said, **"Say ye of him, whom the Father hath sanctified, and sent into the world, Thou blasphemest; because I said, I am the Son of God?"** John 10:36

In Matthew 27:43, the Jews cried out, **"He trusted in God; let him deliver him now, if he will have him: for he said, I am the Son of God."** (John 9:35-37

"Dost Thou Believe on the Son of God?"

"Jesus heard that they had cast him out; and when he had found him, he said unto him, Dost thou believe on the Son of God? He answered and said, Who is he, Lord, that I might believe on him? And Jesus said unto him, Thou hast both seen him, and it is he that talketh with thee."

Jesus clearly told others that He was the Son of God.

God Referred to Jesus as His Son.

"While he yet spake, behold, a bright cloud overshadowed them: and behold a voice out of the cloud, which said, This is my beloved Son, in whom I am well pleased; hear ye him." Matthew 17:5

Scripture Identifies Christ as God's Son

"In this was manifested the love of God toward us, because that God sent his only begotten Son into the world, that we might live through him." I John 4:9

"He that spared not his own Son, but delivered him up for us all, how shall he not with him also freely give us all things?" Romans 8:32

Scripture is full of references to Christ's deity. There are many more verses that confirm Christ as the Son of God, the Messiah, the great I AM.

You might ask, *"How is it even possible for Jesus to be the Son of God and God Almighty at the same time?"*

He's God! **"...With men it is impossible, but not with God: for with God all things are possible."** Mark 10:27

I AM the Messiah

"The woman saith unto him, I know that Messias cometh, which is called Christ: when he is come, he will tell us all things.

Jesus saith unto her, I that speak unto thee am he."

John 4:25-26

There's a lot of debate on whether Jesus is God's promised Messiah, just a prophet, or a fraud. And among the debaters are those who declare that he was just an ordinary man who never even claimed to be the Messiah. So who is right?

What did God say about the Jewish Messiah in His word?

Isaiah 9:6 says, **"For unto us a child is born, unto us a son is given: and the government shall be upon his shoulder: and his name shall be called Wonderful, Counsellor, The mighty God, The everlasting Father, The Prince of Peace."**

Then Luke 2:11 announces the birth of the child mentioned in Isaiah 9:6.

"For unto you is born this day in the city of David a Saviour, which is Christ the Lord."

So the Savior is *also* referred to as **"Wonderful, Counsellor, The mighty God, The everlasting Father, The Prince of Peace,"** and **"Christ the Lord."**

Who is this Messiah and why did God send Him?

The answer can be found in Matthew 1:20-21:

"But while he [Joseph] thought on these things, behold, the angel of the Lord appeared unto him in a dream, saying, Joseph, thou son of David, fear not to take unto thee Mary thy wife: for that which is conceived in her is of the Holy Ghost.

And she shall bring forth a son, and thou shalt call his name JESUS: for he shall save his people from their sins."

So an angel appeared unto Joseph (Mary's betrothed) in a dream and clearly told him that the child, who was miraculously conceived, was to be named JESUS and **"he shall save his people from their sins."** That's why Jesus came into this world – to save us from sin.

Scripture States that Jesus is the Messiah

"One of the two which heard John speak, and followed him, was Andrew, Simon Peter's brother. He first findeth his own brother Simon, and saith

unto him, We have found the Messias, which is, being interpreted, the Christ. And he brought him to Jesus..." John 1:40-42a

He told Peter they found the Messiah and took him to *Jesus.*

Acts 5:30-31 says, **"The God of our fathers raised up Jesus, whom ye slew and hanged on a tree. Him hath God exalted with his right hand to be a Prince and a Saviour, for to give repentance to Israel, and forgiveness of sins."**

Isaiah referred to the Christ Child as the **"Prince of Peace"** while Luke called him the **"Saviour."**

"For God so loved the world, that he gave his only begotten Son, that whosoever believeth in him should not perish, but have everlasting life. For God sent not his Son into the world to condemn the world; but that the world through him might be saved." John 3:16-17

Romans 6:23 says, **"For the wages of sin is death..."** Jesus paid the penalty for our sin. **"...but the gift of God is eternal life through Jesus Christ our Lord."** Salvation is a gift to all who believe. (John 3:16; Ephesians 2:8-9)

Jesus Claimed to be the Messiah

"Then came the Jews round about him, and said unto him, How long dost thou make us to doubt? If

thou be the Christ, tell us plainly. Jesus answered them, I told you, and ye believed not: the works that I do in my Father's name, they bear witness of me." John 10:24-25

"But he held his peace, and answered nothing. Again the high priest asked him, and said unto him, Art thou the Christ, the Son of the Blessed? And Jesus said, I am: and ye shall see the Son of man sitting on the right hand of power, and coming in the clouds of heaven." Mark 14:61-62

- As you can see, an angel announced His birth and called Him the Messiah.
- Jesus claimed to be the Messiah.
- Scripture supports His claim.

The
Knowledge of
God

God Makes No Mistakes

> *"For if our heart condemn us, God is greater than our heart, and knoweth all things."*
>
> I John 3:20

God knows all things.

Life is full of uncertainties and unplanned detours. How do we know which path to take or which decision is the right one when faced with dozens of alternatives while dealing with disobedient children, family disputes, or job challenges. What about financial decisions, legal complications, marital disagreements, or medical problems? The list is endless.

You can consult a professional – a child psychologist, a counselor, a lawyer, or a financial advisor – and many people do. But if they're too costly, just ask your best friend for advice. And many people do that, too.

The problem is that these advisors, regardless of their good intentions or worldly knowledge on a particular subject are extremely limited in their foresight, as are we all. The only one with unlimited knowledge on all subjects is God Almighty.

Isaiah 40:28 says, **"Hast thou not known? hast thou not heard, that the everlasting God, the LORD, the**

Creator of the ends of the earth, fainteth not, neither is weary? there is no searching of his understanding."

Our knowledge is limited by time, space, intelligence, and education. God is not limited by any of those things because He is omnipresent and omniscient. There is nothing that God doesn't understand.

- He knows the secrets and longings of your heart.
- He knows your dreams, challenges, and pain.
- He knows what's best for every one of His children.
- He knows your future.
- He doesn't miss the mark or make errors in judgment like we do.
- He always *tells* the truth. He *knows* the truth. He *is* the truth.

His knowledge and understanding never end.

I John 3:19-21 says, **"And hereby we know that we are of the truth, and shall assure our hearts before him. For if our heart condemn us, God is greater than our heart, and knoweth all things. Beloved, if our heart condemn us not, then have we confidence toward God."**

You might deceive yourself into thinking you're saved and ignore the condemnation of your heart, but God is greater than your heart. He knows if you really belong to Him.

Daniel 2:22 says, **"He revealeth the deep and secret things: he knoweth what is in the darkness, and the light dwelleth with him."**

Regardless of what we say or do or believe, God knows the truth – about our lives, our faith, our thoughts.

Hebrews 4:13 says, **"Neither is there any creature that is not manifest in his sight: but all things are naked and opened unto the eyes of him with whom we have to do."**

God sees and knows *everything*. Nothing can be hidden from His all-seeing eye. God knows your past. God knows your future. And God knows everything you're going through at this very moment. Who better to ask for advice and counsel?

There is an expression, "You get what you pay for."

- Advice from a friend is free, but it could cost you in other ways when you make a wrong decision.

- Advice from a professional is costly and it's not guaranteed to give you clear direction or help you make correct choices, so it could also mislead you.
- But guidance from God can be the most expensive, because He doesn't give advice. Advice is something you can choose to follow or ignore.

First, God only gives directions to those who have committed their lives to Him, and that's a lifetime commitment.

Second, God only instructs those who *intend* to obey Him. And He knows your intentions, too.

You'll never go wrong by seeking His direction and following His guidelines. Whether you understand why or agree with His direction, you'll save yourself a lot of grief by doing it God's way. He makes no mistakes.

God Knows Everything

> *"Talk no more so exceeding proudly; let not arrogancy come out of your mouth: for the LORD is a God of knowledge, and by him actions are weighed."*
>
> I Samuel 2:3

God knows everything.

He knows our actions, our intentions, our goals, our dreams, our desires, our wants, our struggles.

In I Chronicles 28:9, King David said, **"And thou, Solomon my son, know thou the God of thy father, and serve him with a perfect heart and with a willing mind: for the LORD searcheth all hearts, and understandeth all the imaginations of the thoughts: if thou seek him, he will be found of thee; but if thou forsake him, he will cast thee off for ever."**

You see, **"the LORD searcheth all hearts, and understandeth all the imaginations of the thoughts:"**

When I was a girl, my mother used to tell me, "It's the thought that counts." There's a lot of truth in that. The "thought" is my intention, my motive, my reason for doing something.

I can do the right thing for all the wrong reasons, and God knows it. Or my motives can be pure and my intentions honorable, yet someone accuses me wrongly. God knows that, too, because He **"understandeth all the imaginations of the thoughts"** for He is **"a God of knowledge,"** and He knows you better than you know yourself.

When people think they're full of knowledge ... that they have all the answers ... that they know more than others, then their hearts are lifted up in pride. That's when their talk is exceedingly proud and arrogance flows from their lips.

But who can boast in knowing more than God? No one. Our knowledge comes from God. *God gives us knowledge. He doesn't need to take our advice.*

Ecclesiastes 2:26 says, **"For God giveth to a man that is good in his sight wisdom, and knowledge, and joy: but to the sinner he giveth travail, to gather and to heap up, that he may give to him that is good before God. This also is vanity and vexation of spirit."**

Knowledge and wisdom come from God, but He gives travail to the proud and arrogant. **"...for the LORD is a God of knowledge, and by him actions are weighed."**

We have nothing to boast about, for only God can discern the motives and intentions behind someone's actions.

Romans 11:33 says, **"O the depth of the riches both of the wisdom and knowledge of God! how unsearchable are his judgments, and his ways past finding out!"**

Study to Show Thyself Approved

"Study to shew thyself approved unto God, a workman that needeth not to be ashamed, rightly dividing the word of truth."

II Timothy 2:15

There's nothing more rewarding than being approved unto God. When we're approved unto God, we can stand before Him with confidence, knowing that our actions and attitudes please Him. Judgment Day is coming, and we will all stand before God to give an account of our works.

If we are approved unto God, we will hear the words: **"...Well done, thou good and faithful servant: thou hast been faithful over a few things, I will make thee ruler over many things: enter thou into the joy of thy lord."** Matthew 25:21

If you are approved unto God, then Jesus is truly your Lord.

How are we approved unto God? By studying! What are we to study? God's holy Scripture – the Word of Truth. Rightly dividing the Word of Truth means to consider the context and compare Scripture to Scripture to accurately interpret verses.

It's a lot like extracting a couple of sentences out of someone's speech. If we take the right sentences, we can easily twist the meaning of the message. To rightly divide the Word of God, we keep the verse in the context of the entire passage. We don't simply extract a couple of verses from a chapter to make it say whatever we want.

Therefore, when we *study* and *rightly divide* the Word of Truth, we are *approved unto God* and have nothing to be ashamed of.

II Timothy 3:15 says, **"And that from a child thou hast known the holy scriptures, which are able to make thee wise unto salvation through faith which is in Christ Jesus."**

The holy Scriptures are able to make us wise unto salvation through faith in Jesus, so it's imperative we *study* them, *rightly divide* them, and *know* them.

The Spirit of Wisdom

> **"That the God of our Lord Jesus Christ, the Father of glory, may give unto you the spirit of wisdom and revelation in the knowledge of him."**
>
> Ephesians 1:17

Paul encourages the Ephesian believers by letting them know that they are in his prayers.

In verses 15 & 16, he says, **"Wherefore I also, after I heard of your faith in the Lord Jesus, and love unto all the saints, Cease not to give thanks for you, making mention of you in my prayers;"**

What is his prayer for them?

"That the God of our Lord Jesus Christ, the Father of glory, may give unto you the spirit of wisdom and revelation in the knowledge of him:"

When you are saved, the Holy Spirit of God comes to live inside you.

Romans 8:14 & 16 says, **"For as many as are led by the Spirit of God, they are the sons of God ... The Spirit itself beareth witness with our spirit, that we are the children of God:"**

And if God's children choose to live a Spirit-filled life, they allow the Holy Spirit to control their attitudes, their actions, their thoughts, their words, and their lives. That is the Spirit of wisdom, which reveals to us the knowledge of Christ.

God desires to bless each of His children with the Spirit of divine wisdom and reveal to them the knowledge of His Son Jesus. So verses 18-23 follow up verse 17 with knowledge of Christ.

- Verse 18 … God gives us spiritual insight to understand the expectation of His calling and the glorious riches of His inheritance in the saints …
- Verse 19 … God reveals His tremendous power to those who believe, according to the working of His mighty power …
- Verse 20 … Which He used to raise Christ from the dead. Then God set Jesus at His right hand in the heavenly places …
- Verse 21 … Those places are **"Far above all principality, and power, and might, and dominion, and every name that is named, not only in this world, but also in that which is to come …"**
- Verse 22 … God has given Christ authority over everything and made Him head of the church …
- Verse 23 … The church is the body of Christ, who fills it completely.

Without the Spirit of wisdom and revelation in the knowledge of Jesus Christ, a person would miss valuable insight from God's Word, which reveals that knowledge.

God Desires His Children to Grow

"But grow in grace, and in the knowledge of our Lord and Saviour Jesus Christ. To him be glory both now and for ever. Amen."

II Peter 3:18

As much as a mother loves her newborn infant, she desires for that baby to grow up; to one day be a mature adult.

I Peter 2:2 says, **"As newborn babes, desire the sincere milk of the word, that ye may grow thereby:"**

God also wants His spiritual babes to grow into mature believers, and just like with babies, the growth process starts with milk.

The spiritual development of God's children is actually very similar to the physical development of an infant. They both start on milk and if they are growing properly, it's not long before they both start exercising their muscles.

While a baby exercises physically, learning to sit up and crawl and then walk, a believer exercises spiritually, learning to obey and trust God, strengthening his faith.

And while the growth process can be difficult at times, both physically and spiritually, God provides everything we need to grow spiritually – His Word, His Holy Spirit, His church, and His children – other believers who disciple us, encourage us, pray for us, and fellowship with us.

God *instructs us* to grow in grace. That means it doesn't happen by accident. We have to accept some responsibility. But how exactly do we take those first baby steps, strengthen our spiritual muscles, and begin to grow in grace?

We must walk uprightly.

Psalm 84:11 says, **"For the LORD God is a sun and shield: the LORD will give grace and glory: no good thing will he withhold from them that walk uprightly."**

We must purpose in our hearts to cleave unto the Lord.

Acts 11:23 says, **"Who, when he came, and had seen the grace of God, was glad, and exhorted them all, that with purpose of heart they would cleave unto the Lord."**

We must humble ourselves.

I Peter 5:5 says, **"Likewise, ye younger, submit yourselves unto the elder. Yea, all of you be subject** one to another, and be clothed with humility: for God resisteth the proud, and giveth grace to the humble."

We must minister to others as good stewards of God's grace.

I Peter 4:10 says, **"As every man hath received the gift, even so minister the same one to another, as good stewards of the manifold grace of God."**

Just like a father wants his baby to grow up, our Heavenly Father wants His babies to grow up in Christ in every area of their Christian life.

"But speaking the truth in love, may grow up into him in all things, which is the head, even Christ:" Ephesians 4:15

Grow in Grace and Knowledge of Jesus

"For if these things be in you, and abound, they make you that ye shall neither be barren nor unfruitful in the knowledge of our Lord Jesus Christ."

II Peter 1:8

II Peter 3:18 tells us to **"...grow in grace, and in the knowledge of our Lord and Saviour Jesus Christ..."**

God expects our knowledge of His Son to grow. For how can we be more like Christ if we don't know what Christ is like?

When Peter says **"For if these things be in you, and abound,"** he is referring to the character qualities from the previous three verses: faith, virtue, knowledge, temperance, patience, godliness, brotherly kindness, and charity.

We know that by displaying these godly traits we exemplify the love of our Savior, but possessing these qualities also reveals that we've developed an in depth knowledge of our Lord and Savior. When these traits freely flow from the nature of Christ within us, they abound. And when they abound, our knowledge of Christ also abounds.

Barren means more than unable to bear offspring; it means *unprofitable*. Unfruitful also means *unprofitable* or *not producing good results*. Therefore, we don't want to be barren or unfruitful in the knowledge of our Lord and Savior. Because that knowledge leads us:

- to the truth of God's Word.
- to Christ our Creator
- to the Great Shepherd
- to the Bread of Life
- to eternal life.

If these character traits abound in you, they make you *profitable* in the knowledge of our Lord Jesus Christ. In other words, your knowledge of Christ abounds with greater understanding, and you'll begin to recognize Him as the *I AM* of the Old Testament.

II Peter 1:3-4 says, **"According as his divine power hath given unto us all things that pertain unto life and godliness, through the knowledge of him that hath called us to glory and virtue: Whereby are given unto us exceeding great and precious promises: that by these ye might be partakers of the divine nature, having escaped the corruption that is in the world through lust."**

Through the knowledge of Christ, we also receive **"all things that pertain unto life and godliness"** and

"exceeding great and precious promises" that we might be partakers of His divine nature.

II Peter 1:2 says, **"Grace and peace be multiplied unto you through the knowledge of God, and of Jesus our Lord."**

So it's crucial that our knowledge of Christ be not barren, nor unfruitful.

The Voice of God

How to Discern God's Voice

"My sheep hear my voice, and I know them, and they follow me."

John 10:27

Do you recognize the voice of your daughter when she calls to you? How about your son? If you have more than one child, can you distinguish between their voices? Of course you can. And you also know the voices of other close family members – your grandchildren, parents, and siblings; or cousins who grew up with you. You've been listening to their voices day after day; year after year. You'd recognize them anywhere.

But can you identify the voice of God?

If you can't, why not? If you are in God's family, your Heavenly Father speaks to you just like your Earthly father does. He talks to you throughout the day, guiding and directing you; giving you instructions and answering your questions. Do you recognize His voice, or do you ignore Him day after day, week after week, year after year.

Jesus said in John 10:27, **"My sheep hear my voice, and I know them, and they follow me."**

The same way babies learn to recognize the voice of their parents – by listening to their voices, baby

Christians learn to recognize the voice of their Savior – by listening to *His* voice.

But how can I distinguish between the voice of God and the voice of Satan?

That's a good question.

II Corinthians 11:14-15 says, **"And no marvel; for Satan himself is transformed into an angel of light. Therefore it is no great thing if his ministers also be transformed as the ministers of righteousness; whose end shall be according to their works."**

That means that the devil and his emissaries try to imitate God by *looking* righteous while they lead you astray. If they can keep you busy doing good deeds and serving the church, you may happily go out into eternity lost, never knowing that works and church membership *don't save you.*

And don't forget that you also have your own voice, your own goals, and your own desires, which, by nature, contradict everything God would have you to do.

Isaiah 55:8-9 says, **"For my thoughts are not your thoughts, neither are your ways my ways, saith the LORD. For as the heavens are higher than the earth, so are my ways higher than your ways, and my thoughts than your thoughts."**

The Voice of God

Because we think so differently than God, there's only one way that we can learn to discern His voice and that is *through His Word.*

John 17:17 says, **"...thy word is truth."**

The greatest way to discern error is *to know the truth.* People who handle money (such as those who work in a bank) are not taught how to recognize counterfeit bills; they're trained to recognize the real thing.

The same is true about God's truth and Satan's lies. Once you've learned to recognize the voice of God, you'll be able to discern His voice and ignore all others.

The more you know the Word of God – allowing its truth to infiltrate your mind, take root in your heart, permeate your soul, and change your life – the easier it is to recognize God's voice.

A Still Small Voice

> *"And he said, Go forth, and stand upon the mount before the LORD. And, behold, the LORD passed by, and a great and strong wind rent the mountains, and brake in pieces the rocks before the LORD; but the LORD was not in the wind: and after the wind an earthquake; but the LORD was not in the earthquake:*
>
> *And after the earthquake a fire; but the LORD was not in the fire: and after the fire a still small voice."*
>
> I Kings 19:11-12

Sometimes when you want to get someone's attention, you raise your voice so they can hear you, or you might even shout, "Hey! Pay attention. This is important."

But when God talks to us, does He ever tell us something that's *not* important? Does He engage in idle chit chat? Does He raise His voice or shout to get our attention? No. In fact, God whispers. You must listen very closely or you'll miss it.

When Elijah was listening for instructions from God, he discovered that God was not in the powerful wind or the earthquake or the fire. God didn't speak to Him through a destructive force, but through a still, small voice.

And that's the same way He talks to us today.

Isaiah 40:11 says, **"He shall feed his flock like a shepherd: he shall gather the lambs with his arm, and carry them in his bosom, and shall gently lead those that are with young."**

Often, the destructive forces in our lives are due to sin in one form or another. God is gentle and kind, and He speaks to His children in love. That's why He uses a soft and gentle voice.

Our lives today are filled with such incredible noise that we can't hear God's voice – motorized vehicles, traffic, constant chatter, lawnmowers, power tools, electronics of all sorts, and the list goes on. In addition to the racket, we're usually so focused on *our* goals, *our* desires, and *our* plans, that we can't even hear God attempting to redirect us.

I worked as a bus monitor for the Head Start program. If there was a change in routine, no matter how slight, I could call a child by name and repeat my instructions six or eight times, but they did not hear a word I said. They were so focused on what they needed to do, they followed the routine, not the instructions. I had to physically redirect them, and even then, they sometimes resisted the redirection because it was not what they were used to.

So often, God's children respond to His voice like the four and five-year old preschoolers responded to mine. They maintain their focus on their plans, regardless of God's instructions.

"I don't know what God wants me to do. He never talks to me."

God talks to *all* His children. He gives us guidance and instruction throughout the day.

In Matthew 15:10, Jesus **"called the multitude, and said unto them, Hear, and understand…"**

And that's what God expects us to do: *hear and understand.*

To hear my instructions, a child simply needed to stop and listen to my voice.

To hear God's instructions, all we need to do is stop and learn to listen for His still, small voice. You won't hear Him by accident. God doesn't shout above the noise in your life. To hear His voice, you need to be quiet, to be still, and to listen. It is a skill that you can develop if you choose to.

The Voice of God is Power

"The voice of the LORD is upon the waters: the God of glory thundereth: the LORD is upon many waters.

The voice of the LORD is powerful; the voice of the LORD is full of majesty.

The voice of the LORD breaketh the cedars; yea, the LORD breaketh the cedars of Lebanon.

He maketh them also to skip like a calf; Lebanon and Sirion like a young unicorn.

The voice of the LORD divideth the flames of fire.

The voice of the LORD shaketh the wilderness; the LORD shaketh the wilderness of Kadesh.

The voice of the LORD maketh the hinds to calve, and discovereth the forests: and in his temple doth every one speak of his glory."

Psalm 29:3-9

- The voice of God displays His glory.
- The voice of God demonstrates His power.
- The voice of God shows how vulnerable we really are.

No one likes to be weak or helpless or vulnerable, but if you don't ever see your weakness, you won't ever turn to God for strength. And if you never see your sinfulness, you'll never turn to God for salvation.

Psalm 18:2-3 says, **"The LORD is my rock, and my fortress, and my deliverer; my God, my strength, in whom I will trust; my buckler, and the horn of my salvation, and my high tower. I will call upon the LORD, who is worthy to be praised: so shall I be saved from mine enemies."**

The voice of God reminds us of His strength and power - that He is worthy to be praised simply because *He is God.*

The voice of the Lord is full of God's power, might, majesty. and strength. Is there anything too hard for God?

With His mighty voice...

- He spoke the worlds into existence. (Genesis 1:1)
- He brought light into a dark and empty world. (Genesis 1:3)
- He **"divided the waters which were under the firmament from the waters which were above the firmament."** (Genesis 1:7)
- He calmed the sea. (Mark 4:39)

- He raised the dead. (Mark 5:38-42; John 11:41-44)
- He cleansed lepers. (Luke 17:12-14)
- He healed the sick. (Matt. 9:20-22)

Luke 1:37 says, **"For with God nothing shall be impossible."**

- His voice will encourage you.
- His voice will rebuke you.
- His voice will comfort you.
- His voice will strengthen you.
- His voice will guide you.
- His voice will empower you.

Trust the voice of God. He speaks clearly and boldly through His Word, through His Holy Spirit, and through His obedient servants.

Obey the Voice of Jesus

"Whether it be good, or whether it be evil, we will obey the voice of the LORD our God, to whom we send thee; that it may be well with us, when we obey the voice of the LORD our God."

Jeremiah 42:6

It is important to obey the voice of the Lord because He always knows what's right and what is best for us. The children of Israel knew that if they obeyed God that it would be well with them; meaning that God would bless them and take care of them.

Hebrews 13:8 says, **"Jesus Christ the same yesterday, and to day, and for ever."**

God hasn't changed, and Jesus is God.

John 8:58 says, **"Jesus said unto them, Verily, verily, I say unto you, Before Abraham was, I am."**

The great I AM is God Almighty. And if it was well with the Hebrew children when they obeyed His voice, it will be well with God's children today. They will be blessed and cared for. If you are an obedient child of God, it will be well with you.

However, when faced with a dilemma, some Christians seek God's counsel like the lost seek guidance from their friends. They pray, "Lord, I need help. Show me what to do, and I'll do it."

But as they're getting off their knees, they're thinking, *Of course, I always reserve the right to choose not to follow God's instructions if He tells me to do something I don't want to do.*

That's what happened to Judah. The Chaldeans had raided the land and taken captives. In fear and desperation, the remnant went to Jeremiah and begged for him to inquire of God for them.

"That the LORD thy God may shew us the way wherein we may walk, and the thing that we may do. ... The LORD be a true and faithful witness between us, if we do not even according to all things for the which the LORD thy God shall send thee to us." (Jeremiah 42:3,5)

So the men of Judah sent Jeremiah to inquire of God and assured him that they would obey God's voice **"Whether it be good, or whether it be evil,"** meaning they would obey regardless of whether or not they liked his instructions.

Ten days later, Jeremiah returned to them with God's answer. God told them to stay right where they were, and He would rebuild them and protect them from the king of Babylon. Then Jeremiah told them what God would do to them if they left Judah and went into Egypt. (Jeremiah 42:7-18)

I wondered why God warned them against going into Egypt when they displayed such sincerity in their request for God's help. Then I got to the next chapter. (43:2,4)

After Jeremiah gave them God's instructions, he was confronted by **"all the proud men,"** who said, **"...Thou speakest falsely: the LORD our God hath not sent thee to say, Go not into Egypt to sojourn there. ... So Johanan the son of Kareah, and all the captains of the forces, and all the people, obeyed not the voice of the LORD, to dwell in the land of Judah."**

They knew if they obeyed, it would be well with them, but despite what they said, they weren't willing to sacrifice their wills on the altar of obedience.

When God directs us in a way that we don't like, it requires us to sacrifice our wills to Him in order to obey. But if we obey the voice of God, *it will be well with us.*

A Voice from Heaven

"And Jesus, when he was baptized, went up straightway out of the water: and, lo, the heavens were opened unto him, and he saw the Spirit of God descending like a dove, and lighting upon him:

And lo a voice from heaven, saying, This is my beloved Son, in whom I am well pleased."

Matthew 3:16-17

God created mankind to have fellowship with Him: To love and worship Him for all He's done and for all He's given; simply because He's God and He's worthy of our love, adoration, and praise.

But when sin entered the world, that broke our fellowship with God. And as much as God wants to fellowship with us, His holiness cannot associate with sin anymore than life can associate with death.

God is life (John 5:26), but the wages of sin is death (Romans 6:23). Therefore, **"the Father sent the Son to be the Saviour of the world,"** (I John 4:14) giving us the tremendous opportunity to fellowship with Him *through faith in His Son.* That's why **"the gift of God is eternal life through Jesus Christ our Lord."** (Romans 6:23)

219

In our own strength and power, we can never be good enough to please God, no matter what we do. But at Christ's baptism, God confirms that Jesus is His Son and lets us know that He is *well pleased* with His Son. Putting your faith in the Son of God who paid the penalty for your sin is the only way that *you* can please God.

That's why Hebrews 11:6 says, **"But without faith it is impossible to please him ..."**

In the Old Testament, God spoke to his people through prophets.

Numbers 12:6 says, **"And he said, Hear now my words: If there be a prophet among you, I the LORD will make myself known unto him in a vision, and will speak unto him in a dream."**

Even King David sought guidance from God through the prophets or priests. However, I believe there were times when God spoke audibly to some of the Old Testament saints such as Abraham, Samuel, and Elisha.

But in Exodus 33:11, the Bible says, **"And the LORD spake unto Moses face to face, as a man speaketh unto his friend ..."**

Then Deuteronomy 34:10 says, **"And there arose not a prophet since in Israel like unto Moses, whom the LORD knew face to face."**

So we know without a doubt that God spoke audibly to Moses.

But when Jesus was baptized, God spoke from Heaven, not *to* His Son, but *to those* attending the baptism. His words were meant to publicly magnify Christ; to let the world know that Jesus was His beloved Son in whom He was well pleased.

Hearing the Voice of God – A Testimony

God talks to His children throughout the day, but do we listen? Communication is two way. If two people are both talking, and neither is listening, there is no communication between them, and neither knows what the other is saying, because they are both too busy talking to do any listening.

Do you talk to God throughout your day? Do you take the time to listen to Him when He answers you? God enjoys talking to us, too. And I think it must sadden Him greatly when we ignore Him.

Ever since I can remember, I've talked to myself – all day, every day.

At age 17, I accepted Jesus into my heart as my Savior, and immediately, I quit talking to myself and started talking to God. And God often responds.

Not audibly. He speaks in a still, small voice that comes in the form of a thought, and if you're not listening for it, you'll miss it. So when I say that God spoke to me, that's what I'm talking about; not an audible voice.

God's commands have helped me to mature in life

When I was first married, if I didn't get my way about something, I pouted big time. One day, God said to me, "Knock it off!"

Sometimes, God has to raise His voice to get our attention. I never pouted again. I matured some that day. God's instruction has guided me toward spiritual maturity.

When I was young in the Lord, He started dealing with me about my need to be baptized, but I resisted. In fact, I downright argued with Him. I said, "Lord, I was already baptized."

God replied, "Marj, you were baptized because they dragged you to the front and dunked you. Now, do it for Me."

I couldn't argue with that, so I willingly got re-baptized. Later, I realized that I wasn't even saved the first time I got baptized.

God's warning has kept me from injury

One day, I was following Floyd to the car dealership. Just as he passed a metro bus that was stopped at a bus stop, God said to me, "Watch that bus. It's going to pull out right in front of you." The instant that thought entered my mind, I hit the brake, and the bus pulled out right in front of me. Had the Lord not warned me, the bus would have run into my car as I was passing it.

And sometimes, God simply responds to me

On my way home one day, I was exiting the freeway. The west-bound off-ramp circled around and put me onto the main road without having to turn either direction, and my light was green. But a box truck sitting at the red light of the east-bound freeway off-ramp decided to make a right-hand turn directly in front of me without yielding to on-coming traffic.

Still moving at about 40 mph, with no more than two car lengths between me and that truck, without an opportunity to see if the lane beside me was clear, I jumped over (praying I didn't cause an accident), and shot by the guy who was just now starting to move forward.

I said to God, "Oh, my gosh, Lord. What was that guy thinking?" God said, "He wasn't, or he wouldn't have pulled out in front of you."

God enjoys talking to us as much as He enjoys it when we talk to Him.

- Do you ever talk to God just because He's there?
- To show your gratitude for all He does for you?
- To share a concern or idea with Him, like you would with your best friend?

- To ask Him for wisdom in making a decision that would please Him?

When you talk to God, do you listen for His answer? Do you hear the voice of God? If not, it's time that you start listening.

The Will of
God

How to Know the Will of God

"And be not conformed to this world: but be ye transformed by the renewing of your mind, that ye may prove what is that good, and acceptable, and perfect, will of God."

Romans 12:2

One of the most frequently asked questions is regarding the "will of God." Babes in Christ and spiritually immature believers are plagued by this question.

- "How do I know God's will for my life?"
- "Now that I'm saved, do I change jobs or divorce my unsaved spouse or move to another city?"
- "What does God want me to do?"

What does the Bible teach about the will of God?

It's God's will that we're saved

"Grace be to you and peace from God the Father, and from our Lord Jesus Christ, Who gave himself for our sins, that he might deliver us from this present evil world, according to the will of God and our Father:" (Galatians 1:3-4)

"**But as many as received him, to them gave he power to become the sons of God, even to them that believe on his name: Which were born, not of blood, nor of the will of the flesh, nor of the will of man, but of God.**" (John 1:12-13)

"**The Lord is not slack concerning his promise, as some men count slackness; but is longsuffering to us-ward, not willing that any should perish, but that all should come to repentance.**" (II Peter 3:9)

Once we're saved, God expects us to do His will (obey Him)

"**And he that searcheth the hearts knoweth what is the mind of the Spirit, because he maketh intercession for the saints according to the will of God.**" (Romans 8:27)

"**Not with eyeservice, as menpleasers; but as the servants of Christ, doing the will of God from the heart;**" (Ephesians 6:6)

"**And the world passeth away, and the lust thereof: but he that doeth the will of God abideth for ever.**" (I John 2:17)

How do we know God's will?

The Bible is very clear that we are to do God's will, but how do we know what to do? Believe it or not, it's spelled out in the Bible.

- We're to repent and be baptized. (Acts 2:38)

- We're to study God's Word and maintain close fellowship with one another; that means to be in church regularly. (Hebrews 10:25; Acts 2:42; II Timothy 2:15)
- We're to tithe. (Malachi 3:8,10)
- We're to spread the Gospel to the world. (Matthew 28:19-20; II Peter 3:9)
- We're to live holy and sanctified lives, separate from the world. (I Peter 1:16; II Timothy 2:21;   I Thessalonians 4:3-7)
- We're to look and act differently from the world. (I Peter 2:9-10)
- We're to meditate on God's word and hide it in our hearts. (Psalm 1:2, Psalm 119:11)
- We're to love one another. (John 13:35: John 15:12; I Peter 1:22)
- We're to love our enemies (Matthew 5:43-45)

What is God's will for your life?

God's will is the same for each and everyone of His children. Now, the will of God is different from the plan of God.

God's will involves our spiritual development. Helping us to grow and mature in the things of the Lord. That's the same for all God's children.

God's plan involves our spiritual deployment. God's call on our lives. That's different for each of His children. It's easy to know God's will. Just read your Bible and do what it says. (James 1:22) But to understand God's plan for your life, you must first be doing his will and living a life of obedience.

If you are out of the will of God because you see no need to honor and obey His Word, He won't reveal to you His specific plan for your life. Why would He? He can't even get you to obey Him in the little things.

And anyone who says, "I'll ask God what He wants me to do, and then I'll decide if I want to do it," doesn't recognize that God is in charge. He doesn't answer to us; nor does His work stand still because we're not willing to obey.

- We understand God's will by reading the Bible. Everything He wants us to do is in His Word. If we don't understand the will of the Lord, we're behaving unwisely. Ephesians. 5:17 says, **"Wherefore be ye not unwise, but understanding what the will of the Lord is."**

- If we know what God's Word says, and we don't do it, we're only fooling ourselves. James 1:22 says, **"But be ye doers of the word, and not hearers only, deceiving your own selves."**

- And if we know God's will, and don't obey, we're in sin. James 4:17 says, **"Therefore to him that knoweth to do good, and doeth it not, to him it is sin."**

The Mind of Christ

"And he that searcheth the hearts knoweth what is the mind of the Spirit, because he maketh intercession for the saints according to the will of God."

Romans 8:27

We appreciate knowing that our names are lifted up in prayer by the saints of God.

If you request prayer and the following week someone tells you, "I prayed for you every day last week" how does that make you feel? Valued? Special? Loved? Someone cared enough to remember your special need, whether it was financial or medical or spiritual, and they lifted up your name and need before God's throne of grace.

And because we know there's power in prayer, we like to know that there are lots of people praying for us.

But one name stands out above all the rest. The name of Jesus.

So whether you've got a dozen people praying for you … Or you've shared your request with only one friend … Or no one else knows what you're going through, and you're all alone as you petition God …

Remember that Jesus is there beside you, lifting your name in prayer, bringing your petition to God, making intercession for you according to the will of God.

God searches the hearts of each and everyone of His children. He knows what's in them – pride, selfishness, envy, bitterness or compassion, an obedient heart, a caring spirit, love.

God not only knows what's in our hearts, but He also knows what we need to make us more like His Son. So His Holy Spirit makes **"intercession for the saints according to the will of God."**

Intercession is to intervene on behalf of another. In other words, if you are a child of God, Jesus prays for you. And His prayers *always* align with God's will for your life.

I John 5:14-15 says, **"And this is the confidence that we have in him, that, if we ask any thing according to his will, he heareth us: And if we know that he hear us, whatsoever we ask, we know that we have the petitions that we desired of him."**

Now if Jesus petitions God on your behalf, and He always prays according to the will of God, then His prayers are always answered.

Our prayers don't always align with God's will. For example, we might think we need more money to pay a bill when we actually need to learn how to manage our finances better. We might think we need more authority in the workplace when we actually need to learn to humble ourselves. Jesus knows the mind of the Spirit, so He is able to pray for us in accordance with God's will.

However, Philippians 2:5 tells us, **"Let this mind be in you, which was also in Christ Jesus:"**

God expects us to have the mind of Christ, and that only comes from spending time in His word. If you have the mind of Christ, you will know the mind of the Spirit, and you also will pray according to the will of God. And when you pray according to the will of God, you can be assured that God will hear your prayers and answer them.

Be Fruitful in Every Good Work

> *"For this cause we also, since the day we heard it, do not cease to pray for you, and to desire that ye might be filled with the knowledge of his will in all wisdom and spiritual understanding;*
>
> *That ye might walk worthy of the Lord unto all pleasing, being fruitful in every good work, and increasing in the knowledge of God;"*
>
> Colossians 1:9-10

I John 5:14-15 says, **"And this is the confidence that we have in him, that, if we ask any thing according to his will, he heareth us: And if we know that he hear us, whatsoever we ask, we know that we have the petitions that we desired of him."**

When the apostle Paul prayed for the Colossians, he was praying according to the will of God. It was God's will for the Colossian believers to know His will with all His wisdom and spiritual understanding that they might please Him in all they do. Not only that, but God also desired that they increase in their knowledge of Him. That doesn't apply only to Colossian believers, but to all believers everywhere throughout time.

236

Jesus Christ is the same yesterday, today, and forever. (Hebrews 13:8) What He did for the Colossian believers back then, He'll do for us today. Are you praying for the knowledge and understanding of God's will; for your knowledge of God to increase? That is definitely the will of God for every one of God's children, and He delights in answering that prayer.

In Colossians, Paul tells us to ...

- Be filled with the knowledge of his will in all wisdom and spiritual understanding
- Walk worthy of the Lord by pleasing Him in every way
- Be fruitful in every good work
- Increase in the knowledge of God

These are excellent goals, and God desires for each and every one of His children to pursue them diligently; but they aren't gifts such as a God-given talent or a musical ability. It takes commitment, persistence, diligence, and faith to understand God's will and to increase in your knowledge of God; to walk worthy and be fruitful. It doesn't happen by accident.

Be Filled with the Knowledge of God's Will

To be filled with the knowledge of God's will in all wisdom and spiritual understanding you must diligently seek God's guidance through faithful and consistent prayer and Bible study. You must be obedient to what He shows you and purpose in your heart to listen. If God can't trust you to obey in the little things, He will not reveal to you the big things.

Walk Worthy of the Lord

To walk worthy of the Lord unto all pleasing means that your life pleases God by your thoughts, your actions, and your motives. It means to live a godly and righteous life, separated from the sins of the world.

Be Fruitful in Every Good Work

To be fruitful in every good work is the natural result of walking worthy of the Lord and pleasing Him in all you do. It means that you will accomplish good things for the Lord in everything you do, and they will have eternal value.

Increase in Your Knowledge of God

To increase in your knowledge of God you must be in His Word daily – reading, studying, meditating, searching – for answers, for truth, for wisdom, for God.

Jeremiah 29:13 says, **"And ye shall seek me, and find me, when ye shall search for me with all your heart."**

Search for God with all Your Heart

Searching for God with all your heart requires diligent Bible study, faithful attendance in a doctrinally sound Sunday school class and church service, and earnest prayer time.

If you seriously pursue the knowledge of God's will in all wisdom and spiritual understanding and diligently work to increase in the knowledge of God, you will please God in everything you do and be fruitful in every good work.

Be Transformed by Renewing Your Mind

> *"For ye have need of patience, that, after ye have done the will of God, ye might receive the promise."*
>
> Hebrews 10:36

What promise is he talking about?

Hebrews 10:37 (the very next verse) says, **"For yet a little while, and he that shall come will come, and will not tarry."**

He's referring to the return of Christ and to the promise of eternal life.

Titus 1:2 says, **"In hope of eternal life, which God, that cannot lie, promised before the world began;"**

God keeps His Word. He is completely and totally trustworthy.

Numbers 23:19 says, **"God is not a man, that he should lie; neither the son of man, that he should repent: hath he said, and shall he not do it? or hath he spoken, and shall he not make it good?"**

You can't always trust another person to keep their word or to follow through with their promises, but God will never fail you.

Colossians 3:24 says, **"Knowing that of the Lord ye shall receive the reward of the inheritance: for ye serve the Lord Christ."**

When you are doing God's will, you are serving the Lord Christ, and you shall receive the promise of God, "the reward of the inheritance," which is eternal life.

Doing the will of God is not hard, but it requires a serious commitment to God.

Your child has a will. When your children want to do something that you've asked them not to do, and they obey you, they are choosing to do your will and please you rather than following their own will. When they disobey and do it anyway, they are living in rebellion, choosing *their* will over yours. That's how it works when it comes to doing God's will.

God has given you freewill. And the things you want to do may be contrary to His Word or His specific calling on your life. So you have to make a choice. Just like your child, you need to decide whether or not you will obey. If you disregard God's will, you'll be living in rebellion, choosing your will over His, but if you do God's will, then you choose to give up your own.

In a nutshell, "doing God's will" simply means to obey God. Therefore, doing the will of God is simple, but it's not always easy. God often asks us to do things that we don't want to do (like we do with our children), and that requires us to relinquish our will.

I want to obey God, but I don't know His will.

II Timothy 2:15 says, **"Study to shew thyself approved unto God, a workman that needeth not to be ashamed, rightly dividing the word of truth."**

You will find God's will in His Word. So the best place to start searching for God's will is in His Word.

Romans 12:2 says, **"And be not conformed to this world: but be ye transformed by the renewing of your mind, that ye may prove what is that good, and acceptable, and perfect, will of God."**

Your mind will be renewed only through your submission to the Word of God.

That's why Jesus said in Matthew 4:4, **"...It is written, Man shall not live by bread alone, but by every word that proceedeth out of the mouth of God."**

Absorbing yourself in the Word of God is the only way your mind will be renewed. And renewing your mind through God's Word is the only way that you will know the will of God. **"...that, after ye have done the will of God, ye might receive the promise."**

The Will of God

I John 2:17 says, **"And the world passeth away, and the lust thereof: but he that doeth the will of God abideth for ever."**

In Everything Give Thanks

> *"In every thing give thanks: for this is the will of God in Christ Jesus concerning you."*
>
> I Thessalonians 5:18

God's will for your life is simple. **"In everything give thanks ..."**

Now that doesn't mean *for* everything, but in all circumstances and situations. It also doesn't mean that you're to be thankful in only some situations or circumstances; when you're having a good day or when things are going your way, but it means that you're to give thanks in the midst of trials and troubles.

No matter what's happening in your life, there's always something for which to be grateful, and that's why we're to give thanks.

- You have a serious car accident, but no one is killed.
- You lose your home to a fire, but everyone gets out safely – even your dog.
- You lose your job through corporate lay-offs, but your family pulls together and works together during this difficult time.
- You bury a child or a spouse, but you know you'll see them again in Heaven.

- You (or a loved one) has just been diagnosed with a dreaded disease, but you know that God will guide you through the incredibly difficult decisions you must make.

No matter what you go through in life, there's always something good in which to be thankful. God wants us to focus on:

- the good, not the bad
- the positive, not the negative
- His blessings, not our struggles

James 1:17 says, **"Every good gift and every perfect gift is from above, and cometh down from the Father of lights, with whom is no variableness, neither shadow of turning."**

Everything good comes from God, and that's what we're to be thankful for: the good. A genuine spirit of thanksgiving precedes answered prayer, and we all want to know that God will hear and answer our prayers.

Philippians 4:6-7 says, **"Be careful for nothing; but in every thing by prayer and supplication with thanksgiving let your requests be made known unto God. And the peace of God, which passeth all understanding, shall keep your hearts and minds through Christ Jesus."**

We're to bring our petitions to God with a heart of thanksgiving. Be thankful in all things and humbly come before God in prayer with an attitude of gratitude. *Then* He will bless you with an incredible peace that will permeate both your heart and mind. And that peace is only available through Jesus.

Colossians 3:15 says, **"And let the peace of God rule in your hearts, to the which also ye are called in one body; and be ye thankful."**

You see, God's peace and thanksgiving go hand-in-hand.

Psalm 100:4 says, **"Enter into his gates with thanksgiving, and into his courts with praise: be thankful unto him, and bless his name."**

It's God's will for all His children to be thankful in all things. A thankful heart will give you peace beyond human understanding, and that's something that no amount of money can purchase.

Fire! Fire! - A Testimony

In 1998, two weeks before Christmas, a faulty clock radio cord caused an electrical fire in the bedroom of our 16-year-old daughter, Jamie. Fortunately, Floyd and I were both home when our smoke detector sounded, and so was our son, Toby. But our daughters were both at school.

Toby had been living on his own, and Jamie's dad gave her permission to move into his empty room, so she had been moving her things down the hall to the vacant bedroom. But when Toby came home, he and Floyd hauled her things back to her room and dumped them on her bed and dresser – beautiful lace dresses, expensive porcelain dolls, all her beloved and precious things, some of them irreplaceable like the porcelain doll that Floyd brought her from Germany.

Taking a break from clearing Jamie's things out of Toby's room and moving his things back in, Floyd and Toby were downstairs with me when I heard a strange sound coming from upstairs.

"What's that noise?"

Floyd trotted up the stairs to check it out. It was the smoke detector.

"Fire! Fire! Call the fire department and bring me the fire extinguisher!"

I dashed into the kitchen, grabbed the fire extinguisher, and thrust it into my son's hands.

"Run this up to dad."

Our security alarm system automatically dispatched the fire department, so the moment Toby returned, we went outside to wait for them.

Armed with the fire extinguisher, Floyd battled the blaze and extinguished the flames before the fire department arrived. Then he opened the bedroom window, and thick black smoke poured out of the room.

Our insurance company was grateful because his quick action saved them a lot of money. The fire department would have broken the window that Floyd opened and washed everything down with their fire hose. What the fire didn't destroy, the water would have damaged. So our insurance company readily forked over the money to repaint the room, and replace the carpet and bed.

Jamie was livid. Her precious things had been safe in the other room until her dad and brother moved them. Now, some of her beautiful dresses smelled of smoke.

As for me, I was thanking the Lord for His blessings.

1) Our smoke detector alerted us.

2) We had a fire extinguisher handy.

3) We were home when the fire started. As a result, property damage was minimal.

4) (Our greatest blessing of all.) That electrical cord ran behind Jamie's bed and caught fire to the sleeping bag that she used on her bed as a comforter. Had the fire started in the middle of the night, our daughter would have woken up on fire. As it was, she was safe at school.

To date, we've had two house fires. In both fires, damage was minimal. In both fires, no one was injured. In both fires, God quickly alerted us to the danger. In both fires, God kept everyone safe.

I believe in the goodness of God.

Sanctification

"For this is the will of God, even your sanctification, that ye should abstain from fornication:

That every one of you should know how to possess his vessel in sanctification and honour."

I Thessalonians 4:3-4

God desires our sanctification. Sanctification is a progressive work of divine grace in which the believer is gradually cleansed from the corruption of his old nature, and is presented "unspotted before the throne of God."

How great is that? To stand before God holy and clean. And that is God's will for all mankind. But the sanctification process cannot begin until a person is quickened by the Holy Spirit of God and made spiritually alive. That "quickening" happens the moment a person accepts Christ into his life.

II Thessalonians 2:13 says, **"But we are bound to give thanks alway to God for you, brethren beloved of the Lord, because God hath from the beginning chosen you to salvation through sanctification of the Spirit and belief of the truth:"**

It's God's will to sanctify each and every one of us, and He does that through His Son, Jesus.

It's also God's will that **"...ye should abstain from fornication..."**

This word is used in Scripture to refer to the sin of impurity between unmarried persons, for idolatry, and for all kinds of infidelity to God. Abstaining from fornication is the first step toward sanctification.

"...That every one of you should know how to possess his vessel in sanctification and honour."

To possess one's "vessel in sanctification and honor" means that we are to be in control of our bodies in a way that sanctifies and honors them. Sanctify means pure or free from sin, and honor means to highly respect. How can we highly respect our bodies and keep them pure if we engage in fornication?

So what is God's will for each of His children?

- "Even your sanctification ...
- That ye should abstain from fornication ...
- That every one of you should know how to possess his vessel in sanctification and honour."

The Word of
God

In the Beginning was the Word

> *"In the beginning was the Word, and the Word was with God, and the Word was God."*
>
> John 1:1

We understand the Word of God to be the Bible.

To mankind, "word" means something spoken or written. We fill books and magazines with the words of men. We fill the air with the words we speak. We see a word as nothing more than a means of communication. And the Holy Scriptures *is* the written Word of God, bound by a cover. We refer to it as the Holy Bible. Hence, the Bible is the written Word of God.

All Christians know that the word "Holy" means the Bible is set above all other printed material and is to be revered. Yet, have you considered how much more there is to the Word of God than His Holy Scriptures?

Jesus is the Word that was with God in the beginning.

We know that because John 1:14 says, **"And the Word was made flesh, and dwelt among us, (and we beheld his glory, the glory as of the only begotten of the Father,) full of grace and truth."**

That was Jesus.

I John 5:7 says, **"For there are three that bear record in heaven, the Father, the Word, and the Holy Ghost: and these three are one."**

Jesus is again called the Word.

"And these three are one" indicates that God the Father and the Holy Ghost are also the Word.

However, in John 10:30, Jesus professed Himself *to be* God when He said, **"I and my Father are one."**

And we are all familiar with John 3:16, which says, **"For God so loved the world, that he gave his only begotten Son, that whosoever believeth in him should not perish, but have everlasting life."**

We know it says that God gave His Son that we might be saved. But do you realize that I John 3:16 says that God died for us Himself?

"Hereby perceive we the love of God, because he laid down his life for us: and we ought to lay down our lives for the brethren." (I John 3:16)

Since the Bible refers to Jesus as the Word and declares Him to be God, then the Word of God includes God's written Word (the Holy Scriptures), God's spoken Word, and all three persons of the trinity. Therefore, the Word of God refers to more than God's words, but to Christ, who is God Himself.

Referring to our Savior, Revelation 19:13 says, **"And he was clothed with a vesture dipped in blood: and his name is called The Word of God."**

Hide God's Word in Your Heart

> *"Wherewithal shall a young man cleanse his way? by taking heed thereto according to thy word...*
>
> *Thy word have I hid in mine heart, that I might not sin against thee."*
>
> Psalm 119:9 & 11

Titus 2:13-14 says, **"Looking for that blessed hope, and the glorious appearing of the great God and our Saviour Jesus Christ; Who gave himself for us, that he might redeem us from all iniquity, and purify unto himself a peculiar people, zealous of good works."**

God redeemed us from all iniquity to purify us unto Himself, so why do we still sin? We choose to. Don't get me wrong. You still drag around this old sinful flesh, but you are no longer a slave to your old nature because once you are saved, you are a new creature in Christ.

II Corinthians 5:17 says, **"Therefore if any man be in Christ, he is a new creature: old things are passed away; behold, all things are become new."**

Our flesh is still active, and it will drag us through all sorts of ungodliness if we let it. But God has empowered us with the means to control our sinful desires. And that is through obedience to His Word.

I Peter 1:15-16 says, **"But as he which hath called you is holy, so be ye holy in all manner of conversation; Because it is written, Be ye holy; for I am holy."**

God expects His children to live a life of holiness. You cannot do that if you are in sin; and the flesh draws us toward sin. So how do you counter that ungodly appeal?

Psalm 119:9 and 11 says, **"Wherewithal shall a young man cleanse his way ..."**

Basically, that means, *How does a young person clean up his act?* To live a holy life, you must rid yourself of any sinful attitude, thought, or deed. These are the things we must cleanse from our lives to live holy.

"... by taking heed thereto according to thy word..."

To *take heed* means to "pay careful attention to; to obey." *According to* means "in a manner corresponding to (or in harmony with)." Therefore, we cleanse our sinful and ungodly ways by obeying and living in harmony with God's Word.

"... Thy word have I hid in mine heart, that I might not sin against thee."

To hide God's Word in your heart means to internalize His truths as spelled out in His Word;

- To accept them
- To believe them
- To trust them,
- To make them a vital part of your lifestyle.

However, before you can live by the truths in God's Word, you must first *know* His Word.

You must read it, study it, and meditate on it.

As you start *taking heed according to God's Word*, you will also start hiding it in your heart, and God's Word will empower you to resist temptation so you don't sin against Him.

All Scripture is Inspired by God

> **"All scripture is given by inspiration of God, and is profitable for doctrine, for reproof, for correction, for instruction in righteousness:**
>
> **That the man of God may be perfect, throughly furnished unto all good works."**
>
> II Timothy 3:16-17

No one likes to be corrected, but everyone enjoys being right. That's what Scripture does for us. It provides us with sound doctrine, reproof, correction, and instruction *in righteousness.*

When you are righteous, you *know* what's right and you *do* what's right. God intends for Scripture to guide and influence our lives toward holy living that we may be **"perfect and thoroughly furnished unto all good works."**

That means that God will use His holy Scriptures to make us complete in Christ and that He will equip us with everything we need for all the good work He has for us to do.

When the Bible says that **"All scripture is given by inspiration of God,"** it means that God guided the writers to make known through the written word exactly what He wanted mankind to know as a revelation of his mind and will; the writing of *all* Scripture. Therefore, their writings are infallible because God is infallible.

II Peter 1:21 says, **"For the prophecy came not in old time by the will of man: but holy men of God spake as they were moved by the Holy Ghost."**

The Bible may have been penned by many different writers over the course of hundreds of years, but the Author is God Himself. (That's why it's called the Word of God.)

And it is profitable

- *for doctrine ...* to teach us the truth about our origin, the origin of sin, God's plan for salvation, Judgment Day, and prophecies yet to be fulfilled.
- *for reproof ...* to reveal our sinfulness and show us the way to salvation.
- *for correction ...* to draw us out of sin and guide us toward a holy lifestyle.
- *for instruction ...* to help us live in a way that pleases God.

If we allow God's Word to penetrate every area of our lives, God's righteousness will shine through us.

Romans 15:4 says, **"For whatsoever things were written aforetime were written for our learning, that we through patience and comfort of the scriptures might have hope."**

Everything in God's Word is there to guide us in some way.

II Timothy 2:15 says, **"Study to shew thyself approved unto God, a workman that needeth not to be ashamed, rightly dividing the word of truth."**

God gave us His Word **"That the man of God may be perfect, throughly furnished unto all good works."**

May God's Word light your path each and every day.

God's Word Illuminates Your Path

"Thy word is a lamp unto my feet, and a light unto my path."

Psalm 119:105

God's word shines at my feet and illuminates the spiritual path before me so I can see clearly where I'm walking. The Word of God is *that* light.

The Word of God lightens your spiritual surroundings. It illumines your mind to the things of God and opens your heart to receive His warnings, His mercy, His salvation, and His correction. Without the light of His Word, you'd walk in total darkness. You'd easily stray from the right path, stumble, and fall into sin.

That's why Psalm 119:105 says, **"Thy word is a lamp unto my feet, and a light unto my path."**

The sun lightens our physical surroundings, and total darkness is the absence of *all light.* If you've ever been in a room so dark that you couldn't see your hand in front of your face, you'll understand. You can't walk in total darkness. You'd trip and stumble and fall. You need some type of light to see where you're going.

In Matthew 15:14, Jesus said, **"Let them alone: they be blind leaders of the blind. And if the blind lead the blind, both shall fall into the ditch."**

Why? Because they're walking in total darkness, and they're unable to see where they're going. The same is true spiritually. People everywhere are trying to get to Heaven through some other means than Christ.

Yet, Jesus said in John 8:12, **"... I am the light of the world: he that followeth me shall not walk in darkness, but shall have the light of life."**

The light of life does not come through the church or good works or religion or some false god. It comes only through Jesus. Anyone who is trying to get to Heaven any other way is walking in darkness.

II Corinthians 4:6 says, **"For God, who commanded the light to shine out of darkness, hath shined in our hearts, to give the light of the knowledge of the glory of God in the face of Jesus Christ."**

God doesn't want you to walk in darkness. That's why He's given us spiritual light ... the light of His Word ... the light of the knowledge of His glory in the face of His Son ... a light to illumine our paths.

God's Word is Pure

"Every word of God is pure: he is a shield unto them that put their trust in him."

Proverbs 30:5

Psalm 12:6 says, **"The words of the LORD are pure words: as silver tried in a furnace of earth, purified seven times."**

God's Word is pure: everlasting *and incorruptible.*

- It is holy – s*anctified.*
- It is perfect – w*ithout fault or error.*
- It is tried – *tested and found to be absolute truth.*

Psalm 18:30 says, **"As for God, his way is perfect: the word of the LORD is tried: he is a buckler to all those that trust in him."**

Psalm 19:7-11 gives us greater understanding of all that God's Word does for us.

- **The law of the LORD is perfect, converting the soul: the testimony of the LORD is sure, making wise the simple.**
- **The statutes of the LORD are right, rejoicing the heart: the commandment of the LORD is pure, enlightening the eyes.**

- **The fear of the LORD is clean, enduring for ever: the judgments of the LORD are true and righteous altogether.**
- **More to be desired are they than gold, yea, than much fine gold: sweeter also than honey and the honeycomb.**
- **Moreover by them is thy servant warned: and in keeping of them there is great reward.**

Pure means "not corrupt, untainted." Sin has corrupted or spoiled *all* of God's creation. God didn't create weeds or hurricanes or child abuse or wars or famine or meteorites.

Look around at the condition of our planet due to all the natural disasters, lack of rain or extreme temperatures, wildfires, and the depravity of mankind who finds pleasure in performing horrendous deeds of wickedness.

But one thing can never be corrupted by mankind, and that is God's holy, infallible Word.

Revelation 21:1 says, **"And I saw a new heaven and a new earth: for the first heaven and the first earth were passed away; and there was no more sea."**

Why did the first heaven and the first earth pass away? Because sin entered in, and it corrupted all of creation. That's why we deal with "acts of nature," sometimes referred to as "acts of God."

But God made everything perfect – no thunderstorms or meteor showers or tornadoes or hurricanes. He's not responsible for those things. We deal with natural disasters because of sin. So when the first heaven and the first earth pass away, everything corruptible will go with them. God's Word is not corruptible; *it is pure.*

Jesus said in Luke 21:33, **"Heaven and earth shall pass away: but my words shall not pass away."**

God's Word Shall Not Return Void

"So shall my word be that goeth forth out of my mouth: it shall not return unto me void, but it shall accomplish that which I please, and it shall prosper in the thing whereto I sent it."

Isaiah 55:11

God keeps His word; He cannot lie (Titus 1:2). Whatever He says will come to pass.

Numbers 23:19 says, **"God is not a man, that he should lie; neither the son of man, that he should repent: hath he said, and shall he not do it? or hath he spoken, and shall he not make it good?"**

God's Word is *all* true. Now Jesus is the Word (John 1:1,14), and in John 14:6 Christ said, **"I am the ... Truth ..."**

We can trust the Truth. Therefore, we can trust God's Word, from Genesis to Revelation because it is *all* true. There are no mistakes, no errors, no contradictions in the King James Version of the Bible. It was inspired of God (II Timothy 3:16) and divinely preserved down through the centuries to maintain the pure and holy truth of God's Word.

(Unfortunately, all other versions cannot make the same claim because man reworded Scripture to *his* liking. So while all the modern versions *may contain* the Word of God, the KJV *is* the Word of God.)

Romans 3:4 says, **"...let God be true, but every man a liar..."**

So in today's society where we no longer know who to believer or what is true, especially from the media, know for certainty that you will always find the complete and total truth in the King James Bible. God's words all have a divine purpose.

II Timothy 3:16-17 says, **"All scripture is given by inspiration of God, and is profitable for doctrine, for reproof, for correction, for instruction in righteousness: That the man of God may be perfect, throughly furnished unto all good works."**

Scripture is God's written word, intended to give us sound doctrine as well as reproof, correction, and instruction in righteousness. God desires that His children follow in His holy footsteps.

I Peter 1:15-16 says, **"But as he which hath called you is holy, so be ye holy in all manner of conversation; Because it is written, Be ye holy; for I am holy."**

The Word of God

God doesn't just command us to be holy, but He tells us in His word how to live a holy lifestyle – a lifestyle pleasing to Him.

Matthew 12:36-37 says, **"But I say unto you, That every idle word that men shall speak, they shall give account thereof in the day of judgment. For by thy words thou shalt be justified, and by thy words thou shalt be condemned."**

God doesn't make idle (or worthless) threats like we do. His words are not empty.

Hebrews 4:12 says, **"For the word of God is quick, and powerful, and sharper than any twoedged sword, piercing even to the dividing asunder of soul and spirit, and of the joints and marrow, and is a discerner of the thoughts and intents of the heart."**

Unlike our words, which can often be empty and meaningless, God's Word is powerful and it will accomplish God's divine purpose.

The Power of God's Word

"Study to shew thyself approved unto God, a workman that needeth not to be ashamed, rightly dividing the word of truth."

II Timothy 2:15

God is pleased with our efforts when we study hard to gain His approval. What does He want us to study? His Word. We will never be ashamed by studying and learning the Word of God because...

- God's Word is pure. Psalm 12:6 **"The words of the LORD are pure words: as silver tried in a furnace of earth, purified seven times."**
- God's Word is life. John 6:63 **"It is the spirit that quickeneth; the flesh profiteth nothing: the words that I speak unto you, they are spirit, and they are life."**
- God's Word is light. Psalm 119:105 **"Thy word is a lamp unto my feet, and a light unto my path."**
- God's Word is sharp. Hebrews 4:12 **"For the word of God is quick, and powerful, and sharper than any twoedged sword, piercing even to the dividing asunder of soul and spirit, and of the joints and marrow, and is a**

discerner of the thoughts and intents of the heart."

- God's Word is everlasting. I Peter 1:25 **"But the word of the Lord endureth for ever. And this is the word which by the gospel is preached unto you."**

- God's Word is a saving power. Romans 1:16 **"For I am not ashamed of the gospel of Christ: for it is the power of God unto salvation to every one that believeth; to the Jew first, and also to the Greek."**

And God stands by His Word.

Isaiah 55:11 says, **"So shall my word be that goeth forth out of my mouth: it shall not return unto me void, but it shall accomplish that which I please, and it shall prosper in the thing whereto I sent it."**

Romans 15:4 says, **"For whatsoever things were written aforetime were written for our learning, that we through patience and comfort of the scriptures might have hope."**

When we study God's Word, rightly dividing it, we compare Scripture with Scripture and look to God for instruction and wisdom to understand the things He wants us to know.

- *God's Word is infallible.* It is the Word of Truth.
- *There are no contradictions in God's Word.* It is reliable.
- *The Holy Spirit of God is the teacher.*

John 16:13 says, **"Howbeit when he, the Spirit of truth, is come, he will guide you into all truth..."**

Notice that He's called "The Spirit of Truth." And He will guide you into all truth. The only place on earth where you can find "all truth" is God's Word. (Not a book about God's Word.)

You can only believe about fifty percent of what you read in the newspapers. That means that at any given time, the article you are reading is peppered with errors. So how do you separate the truth from fiction? Without investing the time to research the facts yourself, you will pick and choose what you think is true and what is fabricated.

That's true about conversations, documentaries, magazine articles, books. Even the well-written and well-researched ones could have mistakes. They were written and produced by a fallible human being, so they might have errors in them. The only place that you can find all truth with certainty is *in the Bible,* so what's keeping you from that truth?

In Matthew 4:4, Jesus said, **"... It is written, Man shall not live by bread alone, but by every word that proceedeth out of the mouth of God."**

If Jesus declares that we need **"every word that proceedeth out of the mouth of God,"** that tells us that it's vital that we know the truths in God's Word. That will only come from studying it and allowing God's Holy Spirit to teach us. Filling your life with "all truth" will never bring you shame.

Colossians 3:16 says, **"Let the word of Christ dwell in you richly in all wisdom; teaching and admonishing one another in psalms and hymns and spiritual songs, singing with grace in your hearts to the Lord."**

- Study God's Word.
- Know God's Word.
- Understand God's Word.
- Apply God's Word.

Your Eternity
Awaits

Do You Know Jesus?

"For this is good and acceptable in the sight of God our Saviour;

Who will have all men to be saved, and to come unto the knowledge of the truth.

For there is one God, and one mediator between God and men, the man Christ Jesus."

I Timothy 2:3-5

Titus 2:11 says, **"For the grace of God that bringeth salvation hath appeared to all men."**

God is perfect, and He created mankind in His image.

Adam and Eve, the first man and woman, were created in perfection. They were perfect because God their Creator is perfect. And because of God's holiness, He cannot have fellowship with sinful people.

So when Adam and Eve sinned, all of God's creation immediately fell into a sinful state, and all babies were born with a sinful nature.

Romans 5:12 says, **"Wherefore, as by one man sin entered into the world, and death by sin; and so death passed upon all men, for that all have sinned."**

As a result, we were separated from our holy Creator.

Romans 3:23 says, **"For all have sinned, and come short of the glory of God."**

Then Romans 6:23 says, **"For the wages of sin is death ..."**

Sin has a penalty – Death.

Everyone dies physically. *That's the first death.*

Revelation 20:14-15 says, **"And death and hell were cast into the lake of fire. This is the second death. And whosoever was not found written in the book of life was cast into the lake of fire."**

The second death is an eternal death.

You see, God created us to have fellowship with Him, so he doesn't want us to experience that second death. Therefore, He sent His Son to pay the penalty!

Romans 6:23 says, "For the wages of sin is death; but the gift of God is eternal life through Jesus Christ our Lord."

I Corinthians 15:3-4 says, **"For I delivered unto you first of all that which I also received, how that Christ died for our sins according to the scriptures; and that he was buried, and that he rose again the third day according to the scriptures."**

And God wishes none should perish. Not even you! So he made a way for you to escape eternal damnation in hell.

"For God so loved the world, that he gave his only begotten Son, that whosoever believeth in him should not perish, but have everlasting life." John 3:16

All You Have to do is Confess and Believe

Romans 10:9-10 says ...

"That if thou shalt confess with thy mouth the Lord Jesus, and shalt believe in thine heart that God hath raised him from the dead, thou shalt be saved.

For with the heart man believeth unto righteousness; and with the mouth, confession is made unto salvation."

Only those who accept Jesus as their Savior will have their names written in the Book of Life. It's not a book of the names of every soul who's ever lived. No. It's God's Book of Eternal Life, containing the names of every soul who's trusted His Son as Savior.

But How Do I Get Saved?

1. Admit that you're a sinner and that you can't save yourself. (Romans 10:9-10)
2. Believe in the Lord Jesus Christ. (Acts 16:31)
3. Repent of your sins. (Mark 1:14-15)

Romans 10:13 **"For whosoever shall call upon the name of the Lord shall be saved."**

Hebrews 9:27 **"And as it is appointed unto men once to die, but after this the judgment."**

We'll all face God on Judgment Day. But you want to face Him clothed in the righteousness of Christ. Because anything else will condemn you to hell.

Other Books Written by

Marjorie Strebe

Another, Day, Another Challenge: The Biography of a Child with Williams Syndrome (Third Edition) is about a special needs child who was falling through the cracks of every service designed to support her needs.

Michelle deals with developmental delays and a mental handicap, but she talks very intelligently. Yet most people can't see past her intelligence to her learning disability.

Treasures in My Spiritual Hope Chest, Volume 1

A King James devotional book with scripturally-sound lessons to help you grow spiritually when you read, understand, and apply God's Word to your life. You will discover priceless nuggets of God's truth in each devotional.

Skip Shaughnessy in Keeping Secrets

Still dealing with the murder of his father, rookie cop Skip Shaughnessy (pronounced Shawn-i-see) is plagued by anger, nightmares, and unforgiveness.

But when he apprehends the most wanted heroin dealer in the state of Wyoming, he's targeted by a drug gang who wants him dead, and he starts to fall in love with the adoring young girl who's father actually pulled the trigger.

Skip Shaughnessy in
The Truth Shall Make You Free

Far from home. In possession of fictitious ID. Rookie cop Skip Shaughnessy aids a couple of stranded teenage girls and is accidentally injured on their property.

When he wakes up in their dad's massive estate with no recollection of his identity or his past, he finds himself falsely accused, threatened, and physically attacked. But despite amnesia, Skip has a way of influencing the lives of everyone he touches.

Website: www.marjiestrebe.com

Email: kjvwriter@marjiestrebe.com